WARBIRDS WORLDWIDE

WARBIRDS TODAY SERIES No.2 MUSTANGS

EDITORIAL
Editorial Director/Publisher: Paul A. Coggan

Editorial Address: P.O. Box 99., Mansfield, Notts NG19 9GU, ENGLAND
Tel: (0623) 24288 Fax(0623) 22659

Design Consultant: John M. Dibbs

Contributors:

Gary Brown (UK)

Joe Cupido (USA)

Robert DeGroat (USA)

John Dibbs (UK)

Erich Gandet (Switzerland)

Alan Gruening (USA)

James Kightly (UK)

Lee Lauderback (USA)

Norman Lees (UK)

Derek Macphail (UK)

Frank Mormillo (USA)

Richard Paver (UK)

Dick Phillips (USA)

Chrisian Schweizer (Switzerland)

Scott Sherman (USA)

Michael Shreeve (UK)

Doug Schultz (USA)

Darrell Skurich (USA)

Eddie Toth (USA)

Thierry Thomassin (France)

Elmer Ward (USA)

Front Cover Photograph: Norman Lees in the Intrepid Aviation Company's P-51D N51RR/44-74008 airborne from Duxford in the Autumn of 1991 (John Dibbs). Back Cover: The classic shape, the beautiful curves and the immaculate skin. Who can fail to be turned on by such beauty (and that's just the Mustang?) (Courtesy Anders Saether, Scandinavian Historic Flight) Inside Front Cover: The Old Flying Machine Company Mustang G-HAEC airborne from Duxford (John Dibbs)

CONTENTS

*Photo Captions pages 4 and 5: Page 4 **Top** - Intrepid Aviation's P-51D N51RR with Norman Lees at the controls - article on Page 16 (John Dibbs). **This page:** Top Mustang in the jig at Tri-State Aviation- article on Page 50. **2nd Top:** Stallion 51's TF-51D articles pages 41 and 58. **2nd Bottom;** N1051S - based in the UK and part of the European scene- article on Page 68 (John Dibbs).**Bottom** - John MacGuire's TF-51D (Darrell Skurich) with Vintage Aircraft - article Page74.*

N51N when it was owned by the late Burns Byram (see The Best Years of Our Lives on Page 78) It later became C-FBAU with the C.W.H.

The intention of this introduction is to cover, very briefly, facets of the P-51 story which are quite well known and then go into more detail on some areas which have never been covered, or if so, incompletely or incorrectly.

It is known that the P-51 was ordered by the British and not the U.S. Air Corps. The first aeroplane was built in less than 21 days. By the time production ended, some 15,686 P-51s had been built, making it one of the most widely produced fighters even though it started a couple of years after some of the other fighters. It's victory ratio throughout World War II was 6:1. It was the only fighter to score victories over the Me 262 jet fighter. It's introduction, performance and it's manoeuvrability came at a critical part of World War II. When the tactics were changed from just bomber escort to bomber escort plus beating up anything in sight on the way home, the Luftwaffe was practically eliminated and the bombing along with the tremendous push by the ground forces hastened the final victory.

The Mustang also went on to a sterling performance as a long range escort in the Pacific. It was used at the start of the Korean War until other aeroplanes, such as the F-86 could be brought in. It lead to the P-82 version, the twin Mustang, which had really outstanding performance and manoeuvrability in spite of it's possibly unusual appearance. A detailed study, too long to present here, has shown that the

Edward J. Horkey, Chief Aerodynamicist on the P-51 dissolves some popular myths about the types development and explains why the Mustang was so successful

P-82 approach of two bodies in place of three on a wing was very sound. The reduction on overall frontal areas and interference drags are obvious.

Now for some detailed information. In mid 1938, the British had ordered Harvard trainers from North American Aviation. In those days, people guaranteed the weight and performance of their aircraft, and there were serious penalties if some of these items could not be met. The guaranteed high speed on the Harvard was 206mph and all the performance items had a +/-1% tolerance. This gives a number of 206-2.06 or 203.94 (rounded off to 204 by the British). For some unknown reason, we could not get the first Harvard much over 200 mph. The problem was serious. There were possible changes that would pick up these 4mph, but there were 50 production aeroplanes and more behind the first one, so no major changes were allowed. We were in a panic for two straight weeks.

Personnel worked seven days a week, ten hours a day and night shift was in there help-

ing also. Finally, some minor changes on the canopy gave a little better sealing. The carburettor then had two settings, automatic-lean and automatic- rich. At the high powers in automatic-rich, it was possible to do some powerplant modifications. Finally, a number between 204 and 206 was reached. It sounds easy now on paper, but in those days, it was a crisis. One night, we even waxed the damn flight test aeroplane, knowing that if we got caught, it wouldn't be allowed. The point of this story, however, is that from this diligence, the great production performance and meeting of schedules and the quality control by all of North American, the British were convinced that North American had a lot on the ball. I would like to think that this meeting the guarantees helped considerably when time came to consider support for North American for the P-51 development and production.

Articles keep being published that repeat the old, tired claim about the inputs of Curtiss-Wright in the development of the P-51. In particular, XP-46 wind tunnel data (obtained by Atwood and Kindelberger with tongue-in-cheek to satisfy some British or Air Corps worriers). I was in complete control of all aerodynamic and wind tunnel data used and developed for the P-51. I found the Curtiss-Wright data to be obsolete and very amateurish and of no help. I remember spending only a few hours to scan it. Their wind tunnel people were not yet onto measuring control surface hinge moments, ducts pressures and airflows, power-on effects, etc.

The main point here is that North American, prior to this time, had gone ahead and beefed up their scientific capabilities. The industry was full of what you might call the old designer draughtsman types, and many of them were outstanding. There were plenty of them at North American who worked well with the new scientific world coming into business. North American gave practically free rein to the inputs of the scientific and technical staff. By the end of the war, not only had aerodynamics and thermodynamics and other similar departments been beefed up, but an entire technical section was created.

The people involved here, including Ph.Ds. and others, numbered over 900. It has become apparent that the emphasis on Curtiss inputs to North American are probably presented by the people trying to cover the initial Air Corps lack of understanding of and appreciation for the developments. The Air Corps at the start of World War II, as well as Curtiss, suffered from a lack of scientific talent. However the Air Corps solved this during World War II and brought aboard many fine technical and scientific people (Courtland Perkins, Bob Hage, Bob Ruegg, Jack Gibbs, Joe Flatt, Paul Bickle, just to name a few).

Before leaving this subject, todays perspective brings forth another thought. The lack of Air Corps presence in the early P-51 activities was probably a blessing in disguise. The Wright Field S.P.O.(Systems Project Office) was only two or three people. Rapid decisions were made, sometimes over the telephone. By contrast, the B-2 S.P.O. has numbered over 200 people. The authoritative *Aviation Week* magazine has reported, over a year after first flight, that a maximum altitude of 30,000 feet and a level flight speed of over 300 knots have been obtained. (My God, we did better than this in the first week of flying the XP-86). And all this at a projected cost of close to $1,000,000,000 per aeroplane.

Rolls Royce started World War II with an appreciation of science and engineering that matched North American's and gave a team that accomplished so much. Everyone should read the book *Not much of an Engineer* by Sir Stanley Hooker. He started as an aerodynamicist on the Merlin Supercharger and sparked the marriage and growth of aerodynamicists, scientists, designers, draughtsmen, engineers, testers, etc., not only for the Merlin and Griffon piston-driven engines, but also a series of very successful turbines engines.

There were two basic and powerful scientific breakthroughs in the P-51 development. One was the boundary layer air bleed and the radiator duct. This is shown in Figure 2. Some small auxiliary equipment might have used boundary layer air bleed prior to the P-51, but this was the first time where it was really used in a situation involving a large flow of air. Here, again, a Britain, Meredith, had projected and analysed an effect where air was brought in a duct, expanded efficiently to give more dwell time for each molecule of air to pick up more heat from the radiator, and then was squeezed down to give some thrust. The net effect was good cooling with very little drag. However, it also took the boundary layer bleed to make it all work.

The wing story has been brought up by the media, mostly without having checked out with any of the people who had actually been working on it at the time, and so it has never been very accurate. The truth of the matter is that NACA had come up with the theory and had actually built a 20% thick wing for testing in a wind tunnel, and it looked very good. North American, with the initial help from Robinson and Hartman of NACA, had to develop their own ordinants and abscissas for the 16% thick root and 11% thick tip, just in case, if the laminar flow didn't work, they wouldn't be stuck with too thick a wing. Once the airfoil ordinants were driven for the desired pressure distributions, wind tunnel data were obtained from *Cal Tech* and the *University of Washington* (used to test effect of squared tips). Excellent drag values and good lift and stall characteristics were indicated. Please review Figures 3 to 6. From then on, the spirit from shop people up to Kindleberger was 'This looks great, let's go all out." Thoughts of a conventional 23000 Series airfoil wing back-up disappeared.

After World War II, the thought came to mind that we had done a fantastic job coming up with the laminar flow wing airfoils, that in various forms became and is today an industry standard. Again, showing interdependence of the British and the American scientists, Von Karman wrote a paper where he pointed out that Sir George Cayley, the British aerodynamicist, back in 1799-1826 measured the equivalent ordinants of a trout fish. Von Karman then compared them to a laminar flow airfoil. Closer investigation reveals this is not just close, it's right on. All we smart scientists had done is reinvented what God had done many milleniums ago.

We do not leave the wing story here though , because a unique feature of the laminar flow airfoil with the maximum thickness moved rearward, compared to a conventional airfoil, a flatter pressure distribution curve with lower negative pressures on top,(which means lower velocities) was obtained. Therefore, the flow went sonic at a lower aeroplane Mach number, and the shock wave was well back. The characteristics of the P-51 in terms of Mach number were superior to any of the other aeroplanes available by any country during the war. It was limited to .82 to .83 Mach number, but this was understood because of the thickness of the wing, use of the fabric surfaces, and many other reasons that did not indicate to North American, at all, that there was some kind of magic barrier out there.

A British wind tunnel tester, back in 1935,had said that the wind tunnels had a sonic barrier. The media, with their ignorance and perpetual quest for sensationalism, came out saying, "There's a sound barrier in the air that man can never break through and is afraid of." Well, I don't know anyone at North American who was afraid of such a barrier. We had available, not only high sub-sonic data, but low supersonic data which is available from bullets and projectiles, and we had a pretty good idea that Mach 1 was just another point on a curve, and with the proper design wouldn't present any problems. This coincidence was considerably enhanced when the NACA at Langley Field came up with the clever idea of converting the P-51 wing into a free flight wind tunnel. There was no worry about the wind tunnel wall corrections, and it gave us good data - it was seen that when the aeroplane went say from .6 to .8 Mach number, the flow over the wing was going from say .8 to 1.4. Data points were collected in a very smooth curve. In addition, it was possible to test the effects of sweep. The straight wings used were quite thin; much thinner than the original P-51 wing. The swept wing, of course, showed advantages.

When it came time to building the XP-86, the above background and the impetus of the captured German data, indicated also that sweep was the way to go. North American had generated over 200,000 engineering man hours on the straight wing F-86 but changed to a wing sweep back of 35 degrees at the 25 percent chord line. So in spite of all the garbage from the media in the early part of November, 1947, George Welch, in an XP-86, went Mach 1.02, 1.03 in a slight dive, on the same radar theodolite measuring range at Edwards that had been used by the X-1 for their going in excess of Mach 1 in about the middle of October. Now, if North American was so afraid of the sonic barrier, how could they have a production aeroplane ready and in flight that could go supersonic in a shallow dive so soon after the X-1? Here again, the media covers up this event so as not to decrease the sensationalism associated with the great sonic barrier. The bottom line is that not only was the P-51 a scientific enhancement in it's time, but it was also of valuable help in establishing sweep and the 'scientific sonic slip'.

It is humbly stated that the P-51 with the Merlin engine was a wonderful scientific and engineering thing of both visual and acoustical beauty (short cassette tapes featuring Merlin sounds is available in the U.S.A.). However it's greatest tribute can be found in the fact that the total number of flying machines (both full and large scale such as 3/4 to 1), is steadily increasing through restorations and construction of new machines. Yes, there are even Merlin engines still available. "Mustangs Forever, the ONLY way to fly!" **Edward J. Horkey.**

PIONEER AERO SERVICE INC.

Elmer Ward writes about his lifelong experience in aviation and his company **Pioneer Aero Service** run with son Bret at the warbird haven at Chino, California. **Exclusive Photography** by **Joe Cupido** and **Thierry Thomassin**

I t is difficult to say where *Pioneer* came from without some background on where I came from and my relationship to aircraft. Growing up near Cleveland Airport in the '20s and '30s left me with an interest in aviation which has never dimmed. How could one not be impressed watching Lindbergh land at Cleveland in the *Spirit*, and the massive crowd surging around the aircraft, forcing him to shut down in the middle of the field.

Cleveland was also home to the *National Air Races* most of those years. Who would forget the Travel Air Mystery Ship easily out running all of the latest military aircraft, or the great aerobatics of Al Williams, Harold Johnson, Milo Burcham, Dick Grannier and so many others - but this could go on too long.

In 1940 I left Cleveland for Glendale, California, to attend Major C.A. Moseley's *Curtiss Wright Technical Institute* located at the Old Grand Central Airport. Grand Central was the commercial airport for the Los Angeles at that time, as well as home base for the likes of Howard Hughes and his racer, DC-5, Round the World Electra and prospered Round the World Boeing Strato Cruiser. (Project stalled by the start of WWII). My plan was to get a technical education and then work at North American on the P-51. Such was not to be, however, and I spent the war years at the *Engine Research Laboratories* for NACA back at Cleveland Airport. There I worked on the design of wind tunnels and engine test facilities, followed by test call work on a variety of American and German engines.

All Photographs by Joe Cupido. **Inset Top Left:** Elmer Ward making some final notes before the test flight of Warbirds of Great Britain's new North American TF-51D N7098V/44-73871from Chino in October 1991. **Lower Left:** Straight out of the paint shop, again for Warbirds of Great Britain is P-51D Shangri-La, registered N513PA/44-72934. It is painted in the colours of Don Gentile's famous war-bond drive aircraft which was paraded around the United States in an effort to raise funds. Few photographs of the original aircraft survive except for shots of the nose section. **Above:** in a stock silver paint scheme, representative of one of the aircraft modified by Temco the TF-51D was due

to arrive in the UK as this publication was going to press. **Insets this page: Right:** Nose artwork was prepared by specialist artist Larry Fator of Quicksilver. The detail in the artwork is shown to advantage in the shot below. **Lower LH inset:** The rear cockpit of the TF-51D is painted in a light grey paint scheme with a black instrument panel. Note that the Pioneer Mustang has a varnished wooden floor in the front cockpit and a stainless steel floor in the rear (or passenger seat on the single control D Models). The high standard of work and attention to detail is evident in all these photographs. Our thanks to Pioneer and to Messrs. Douglas and David Arnold for their help and permission.

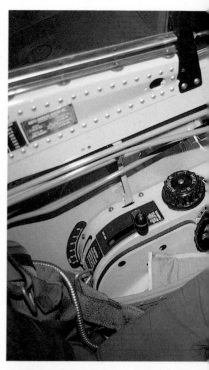

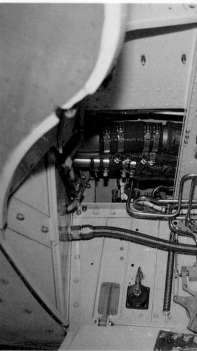

Post war returning to California to further my education at the *California Institute of Technology* while working at the Gugenheim Aeronautics Laboratory (GALCIT) . I had a great time at *Cal Tech* for eight years and ended up going into business designing and manufacturing components for aircraft and military vehicles. The business was sold out from under me in 1977, and I started all over again with *Able Corporation*, which is going strong.

You will note that I had the intention of becoming involved with the Mustang in 1940. Well, it was some years later - 1975 to be exact - before things settled down to the point that I could acquire and fly one. I had started flying in 1941, then there was a hiatus brought on by World War II, and subsequently getting an education. Eventually I got back to flying, and finally in the

early 1907s bought a T-6 followed by the Mustang in 1975. I usually fly every weekend, and during flight test, every day. No compilation has been made, but 1000 hours flight time would be conservative.

Being an instinctive back up type, I started to gather P-51 spares in 1975, which in those days meant meeting Joe Friedman of *Pioneer Aero Service*, because he was Mr.*Mustang Parts*. When Joe decided to retire he approached me to buy him out. Because there was the strong possibility that others might buy him out and then sit on the parts, I decided to acquire the business and have Bret run it.

In support of *Pioneer*, I subsequently bought the Mustang caches of Lefty Gardner and Gordon Plaskett. This put us in the position of having all the major parts for seven Mustangs

plus some 35 engines and car loads of detail parts. Included were all the drawings for all production models of the Mustang (ie. A through H models), the Temco conversions plus many of the Temco parts, and all versions of the Merlin engine.

Having spent a number of years flying and revising *Man O'War*, it was a short step to contemplate building up what we call the *Pioneer Mustang* from our parts and knowledge. Having made the decision, it was necessary to put together an organisation equipped to carry it out. Tools were the easy part - finding personnel that would meet our standards took a little longer. Today we can say that our people can undertake any element of the reconstruction effort and achieve a superior result.

The *Pioneer Mustang* is upgraded where nec-

replaces the remote compass. All instruments are front mounted, and the panel is matt black with a yellow band to differentiate navigation instruments, just like the original.

Landing gear indication lights include the tail wheel as well as the mains. Warning lights are included for coolant door position, generator, inverter, fuel pressure, and oil pressure.

The left console is essentially stock. On the right side the panel looks like the original but includes extra switches for strobelights, inverter radio master, and boost coil. Also on the right side is a circuit-breaker panel with breakers for each individual circuit in the air craft, 31 in all. Complete new sets of placards finish off the interior.

Seats are standard military bucket type. It is expected that pilot and passenger will wear parachutes. We strongly recommend parachutes for this class of aircraft. Floor varnished wood in the pilot seat area with stainless

steel scuff plates under the rudder pedals. The back seat floor is stainless sheet to resist scuffing.

In the 'D' model the battery is moved from the engine compartment to a position behind the passenger. An access door is installed on the right side of the fuselage and the battery is mounted in a sliding carriage so that it can be easily pulled out for servicing. Relocating the battery has two purposes: it not only results in a lower temperature for the battery, but it also balances the aircraft so that there is no need for weights to be bolted to the rudder spar.

There is no padding, no upholstery, no chrome. This is a military aircraft and it looks like one. The stainless steel hydraulic tubing and fittings are not for show, but for safety and reliability. Those tyres do blow sometimes, and would certainly take out aluminium tubing. The stainless tubing will require less attention.

Radios, communications and navigation are

*Pages 10 and 11 Captions: P10 LH - front Cockpit of TF-51D N7098V. **Top Centre:** Clean, efficient look of LH control console and varnished wooden floor.**Lower Centre:** Wheel well detail - the Pioneer Mustang contrasts greatly with the standard wheel well - it's cleaner and much neater. **Above** (by Thierry Thomassin) N7098V before paint in September 1991- skin work is immaculate. Looks as good in the air as on the ground - N7098V on an evening test flight from Chino with Elmer at the controls. (All by Joe Cupido except where noted).*

essary for safety or performance, but built to retain the military flavour of the original aircraft. An example of the improvements can be seen in the hydraulic system. All tubing in the wheel-well area is stainless steel; Hydraulic fittings are all current MS hardware with stainless steel 'B' nuts and sleeves. No original AC fittings are used anywhere in the aircraft. Tubing routing is modified - runs are straight and parallel with custom made clamps to hold them in position. Right 'angle bends are used whenever possible. Custom stainless steel fittings are fabricated where necessary to adapt to existing hydraulic components. The net effect is a cleaner, safer, more reliable installation.

In the cockpit the instrument panel is almost stock. Only two instruments are changed. An HSI replaces the gyro compass and a dual RMI

Top: Biggin Hill and one of Warbirds of Great Britain's P-51Ds - the first produced by Pioneer Aero - in 352nd FG, 487th FS colours as Petie 2nd - Lt. Col. John C. Meyer's personal aircraft. Two other Mustangs operate with similar colour schemes (Paul Coggan) Below: This time in 4th Fighter Group colours, a more recent project for Pioneer was another P-51D, this time named Shangrila. Elmer Ward is at the controls (Joe Cupido)

King Gold Crown. We use older style tuning heads with drum type readouts to better match the period look of the other instruments. There are two comm. heads, two nav. heads, transponder and ADF if required. DME readout can be accommodated in the upper centre of the panel.

All wiring is done by that artist of the wiring harness, Chuck Gabe. There is no one better. The electrical layout was established on *Man O'War* and has not changed, except as required for dual control applications.

The *Pioneer* process is to complete airframe

and cowls fitted - again, all work being done on a special rotary fixture to make access easy.

When putting a Mustang together, most rebuilders mount the fuselage to the wing as soon as the landing gear is installed. Although that single step gives an impression of great progress, it tends to slow remaining installations. Hydraulic plumbing in the wing requires arms and eyes overhead - not a comfortable position. Any components fitted into the fuselage has first to be carted up into the aircraft followed by working on knees in cramped quarters.

elements as far as practicable in the component stage. For example, the wing is completely plumbed, including fuel lines, tanks and pumps, hydraulic lines and wiring. In the case of Petie,(now with Warbirds of Great Britain at Biggin Hill) we completely painted it. However we discovered that even with pads on the wings, we suffered some paint damage from fitting fillets; so we now paint after assembly to the fuselage.

In a similar fashion, the fuselage and vertical and horizontal stabilizers are completed as individual assemblies. The fuselage is mounted in a rotary fixture for easy access to internal structure for installation of equipment.

Firewall forward is handled the same way. Engine mounts are rehabilitated, cowl formers

Captions this page: Top inset - The Pioneer team, from left to right - 'Rocky' Rockwell, Jimmy New and Bret Ward. Centre and Above - TF-51D N7098V..

Pioneer uses the services of *Cal Pacific Airmotive* for major fuselage modifications. such as dual control conversions and for major wing rebuilds. We have all the normal tools for sheet metal work including hydraulic brake and forming rolls, which enable us to undertake all but major modifications. Jigs have been made for all secondary surfaces, flaps, ailerons, trim tabs, etc., for rehabilitation or build from scratch.

Unlike the typical rebuilder, the *Pioneer Mustang* is built up from parts - not from disassembled aircraft. The parts have numerous origins. Some are North American, or U.S. - built spares; some are Canadian, and some Australian. Many are of doubtful parentage. In the event there is a fitting problem, that usually has to be worked

Pioneer Aero Service Inc.

out. The NAA parts are usually a very good fit; but the same cannot be said for much of the rest. The result is a very time consuming process to reach our standard of workmanship. For example, *Shangrila* had taken 6917 + hours all at *Pioneer*. The dual control version required 7605 hours at *Pioneer* plus the time put in at *Cal Pacific*. You can see the significant difference required for the dual control version. Much of the Temco design was inferior, and had to be reworked to reach an acceptable level.

All of the modifications to the TF have been recorded so that we can reproduce the design as it now exists. In addition, a number of other changes have come to mind and will be incorporated in subsequent aircraft. Safety and reliability are always the prime concern. We have been flying the dual control Mustang and find it to have quite acceptable performance. There was some concern regarding the aerodynamic effect of the extended canopy on rudder effectiveness, especially in the landing configuration; but that has not been significant. The tail comes down easily with complete control; throughout the roundout. The somewhat greater longitudinal moment of inertia requires close attention by the pilot following touchdown to keep the nose going straight, but no real heroics are demanded.

The total number of aircraft assembled by *Pioneer* includes the two P-51Ds and one TF-51 for *Warbirds of Great Britain* plus the Bearcat. The latter machine is well along now and should fly early next year. The company has major parts for another four Mustangs, one of which (a dual control) will be retained for pilot training.

At the present time, the selection of engine rebuilder is a customer option. The engine in *Petie* was overhauled by Mike Nixon's *Vintage V-12's*. For *Shangrila* (the second D model) and the TF model *JRS Enterprises* was selected. The Merlin engine is straightforward in design and reasonably reliable when not pushed too hard. The engine in *Man O'War* is an Air Force overhaul done in 1955. It has been in the aircraft since 1970. Shortly after I acquired the aircraft, the engine developed a bad coolant leak at a transfer tube between the head and bank. I had several spare head and bank assemblies and overhauled a pair to put on the engine. Last year I replaced them with another overhauled set because a valve had mysteriously developed excessive wear on the stem. This engine is still running fine with 1100 hrs. on it.

I believe that good life is a matter of proper lubrication and just taking it easy. We use 46 to 50 inches Hg and full rich for take-off at 3,000 RPM. Climb is 2300 turns and 38 inches. Hg at auto rich setting. Typical cruise is 2200 turns and 32 in Hg in auto lean. This will usually net close to 300MPH true at an altitude of 12,000ft. Altitude may seem a bit high to some but we have a lot of mountains in and around California. On long cross country runs we increase altitude to 20,000 feet, full throttle and

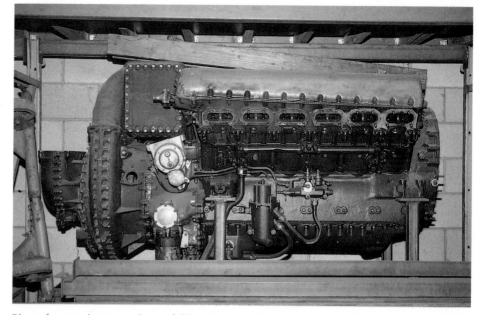

Pioneer has extensive stores and spares holding. Top - One of 25 Merlin engines held by Pioneer. Below: Pioneer's engine test stand in store at Chino. Bottom: Engine heads and banks. The company have a selection of Mustang parts which are replenished on a regular basis. Pioneer can be contacted at Chino on (714) 597 6960 or Fax (714) 597 7550.

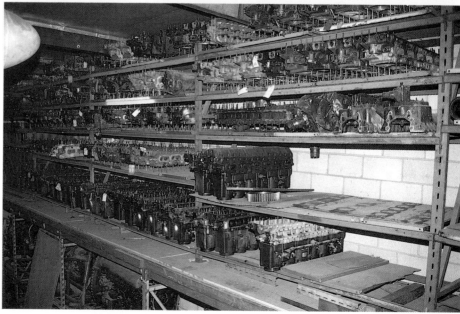

2200 RPM. Manifold pressure is not permitted to go below 18in Hg in low blower.

At the present time we are negotiating with the Chino Airport management for land on which to build a complete facility. We are very cramped and broken up in the present five hangars.In addition to a complete remanufacturing facility, Pioneer will have a flight centre with hangar space for aircraft that we will maintain. All of the normal amenities will be included. It will make an attractive addition to old Chino Airport.

A more detailed shot of a Pioneer Aero Service Mustang cockpit instrument panel - TF-51D N7098V **(Joe Cupido)**

Initial Impressions

Heading Picture: *Norman Lees brings N51RR close in on the camera ship.* ***Above:*** *Norman Lees is currently a commercial pilot for the airline Dan-Air. He has a wide experience of warbird flying both with the Royal*

Norman Lees recalls the experiences of his first flight in the Intrepid Aviation Company's North American Mustang in the United States. Exclusive air to air photography by **John Dibbs**

In November 1989 I had arrived at a small airport in Ohio. Hook Field, Middletown airfield, a few miles to the North of Cincinnati - the home of *Hogan Air* . In amongst the DC-3s and Beech 18s stood two of my three favourite Allied fighters. One, a Hawker Sea Fury stood next to the second, a North American P-51D. The third, which I have subsequently flown is the Spitfire - but that's another story.

One year later, thanks to Robs Lamplough, I was able to return to Ohio, this time to Hamilton, a few miles to the Southwest of Middletown to live a dream of flying the Mustang.

I had visited Hamilton in the Sea Fury and remembered the awkward approach to a narrow runway and the 15 knot crosswind which today was no longer blowing!

Restored by Ron Runyan and completed by *Fighter Rebuilders* at Chino, registered as N51RR/44-74008 is dressed in an early 4th Fighter Group Colour scheme. This immaculately prepared machine stood in the corner of a hangar - normally the home of ordinary business aircraft.

Robs and I had met at Cincinnati airport and now I sat in the cockpit with Robs on the right wing slowly working from left to right around the levers, switches and dials. The cockpit is roomy and if you have flown a T-6 then a few similarities in layout and design are apparent.

Changes from the stock aircraft on which most manuals are based are subtle for the most part. The stick, throttle, flap lever and rudder pedals are still in the same place! In this aircraft switches that were located around the cockpit

Above: Perfect plan view of N51RR hard in the turn in this knife edge shot. **Below:** *Owner David Gilmour against an exciting cloudscape*

are now all grouped together on one panel on the right hand side of the cockpit. We could sit all day arguing the pro's and cons of cockpit ergonomics but you win and lose with some changes from the original design.

The radio and navigation fit have been upgraded and reflect the civilian use;all still within easy reach of the left hand. The original radio control would have been fitted down in the right side, requiring a hand change by the pilot to select a new frequency. Annoying if in formation.

However, on the debit side two important switches normally situated aft and down from the throttle had been moved to the right hand panel.

The Merlin, like the Griffon, is a water-cooled V-12 engine. This P-51 is equipped with a Packard manufactured V1650 dash 7 Merlin but with 600 series transport blocks - (so called because the Merlin 600 engine was utilised in transport aircraft such as the Avro Tudor and DC-4M Argonaut aircraft).

Back to the switches: Oil and coolant temperatures are controlled by regulating the flow of air from the oil cooler and coolant radiator via two shutters. Two four position switches are provided for this purpose. In the AUTO position the shutters are thermostatically controlled and unless oil and coolant temperatures are in the higher part of the green band, both shutters remain closed.

Spiring loaded to off, once out of the auto position the two other selections of Open or Close allow multi position selection as required by the pilot.

Failure of either thermo-stat with any door in the closed position would result in an excessive temperature especially at high power settings; for instance on take off or during a go-around situation in high ambient temperatures.

Close monitoring of temperatures and pressures are a part of any pilots remit but you stand a better chance of radioing a position with both shutters fully fully open in initial stages of flight. On take off if the shutters fail fully closed you will probably lose the engine at around 500 feet! We are again faced with hand changing before joining the circuit in order to open the shutters. You have to hold the coolant radiator

switches for around 20 seconds - a long time when in formation with your hand away from the throttle!

I'm not complaining, but it's worth thinking about. If you fly as a singleton it's not a problem, but the formation situation just makes it difficult. Robs has covered all the controls now and we have reviewed the emergencies and relevant problems of flying the aircraft.

Visibility appears better in the P-51 than the Sea Fury and I think better than the Firefly. You can't see a thing directly in front of you with the tail down in any of these aircraft but visibility to the side of the nose is good in this aircraft.

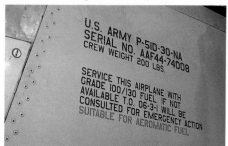

Robs dwells on the go-around. The Sea Fury has such an excess of power and even a late overshoot is not difficult so long as you don't apply the power smoothly and don't use all of it! More boost is required in the case of the Mustang and noticeably more physical throttle movement. With full flap the performance is not so good though 45 inches of boost should be adequate in most cases. The manual says open the power and raise the gear first. Operators seem to be spilt on reducing the flap by 20 degrees first, then retracting the gear. I think the gear should be first in most cases except in the event of a really late go-around, very close to the runway.

One of the other points made was on the gear handle. It's positioning is a little too far forward and I will have to release my harness lock to be able to lean forward to raise and lower. Service pilots were warned not to operate it with their left foot and I can see why they may have been tempted to do so.

Gear handles have been known to break off and many pilots carry a set of mole grips in an effort to cover that eventuality! Using the foot probably meant an undue force being applied before the lever was out of the gate and early handles were made of a magnesium alloy. No one mentioned that the operation was in any way abnormal and why I mention that will become clearer later on!

It was now time to move on and I reluctantly extracted myself from the cockpit - not failing to notice the beautiful lines of the clean laminar flow wing. Beyond the tip lay the hangar floor. I could hardly wait for the view tomorrow which, if the weather held, would be the Ohio countryside!

After a restful night and tasty breakfast at Ron Runyan's home we all drove out to Hamilton. I had read the notes another three times and thought more about the advice given to me yesterday by Robs and by Mark Hanna of the *Old Flying Machine Company* before I left the UK.

Dave Gilmour had arrived to view and fly in the Mustang with the possibility of adding it to his collection of vintage aircraft.

Robs was going to do the first flight - he needed to go to Blue dash a few miles away so suggested I ride in the rear passenger seat. We arrived and Robs disappeared for an hour leaving me to sit in the aircraft once again and go through the cockpit drills one more time. I took time off to look in the hangar which included three immaculate aircraft, a Corsair, T-6 and

Stearman. Once again no landing fee for a warbird visitor. It would be nice if that tradition spread itself across the Atlantic to the East!

We arrived back at Hamilton: not a moment too soon as I was looking forward to my first flight. For the first landing I would head up to Middletown which has a wider runway, only 20 feet but with better approaches I would feel more comfortable. My initial Sea Fury flying had been done from there; over cautious perhaps as I was sure the Mustang would be fine with its wide track undercarriage and steerable tail wheel.

I did my walk-around, secured the rear seat and straps. Once in the front I started to run through the checks. Sweeping slowly from left to right I was now becoming increasingly familiar with the layout. The previous dry runs were paying dividends now. This Mustang is fitted with an oil priming system and even on a warm engine it does not hurt to give it a 30 second burst of oil.

Throttle set, mixture to idle cut off, fuel booster pump on, check pressure, all's well. Locate the priming pump, 3 seconds on a warm engine should be enough.

Both Magnetos on, shout CLEAR PROP, thumbs up from outside, press the starter and the propeller starts to turn. Nothing! No smoke so probably underprimed. Check fuel on, mags on, fuel pressure good. Try another three seconds priming. Don't want to flood it.

Try again: CLEAR PROP. Push the starter - aircraft rocks under the reaction from the turning propeller, small puffs of smoke now and the engine suddenly bursts into life. Mixture control to run. She falters but a burst of primer cures the problems. Oil pressure rising. RPM about 900. Slowly increase the throttle to set 1300RPM.

I look forward through the eleven foot diameter propeller arc. The whole combination is running smoothly. Flaps have moved to up, temperature is rising slowly. I'm ready to taxy .

Quite a crowd has gathered, more to see David Gilmour than to see me fly the Mustang! Throttle back, feet on brakes, wave the chocks away. Talk on the Unicom frequency. I get an answer from the tower. We are both battling with our different accents - the lady is doing better than me!

Release the brakes, edge the throttle open and the aircraft starts to move forward. Check the brakes, all working well. Move the stick forward to unlock the tailwheel. It steers through 6 degrees either side using the rudder pedals but I need to turn through 90 degrees onto the taxiway. Just like the later marks of Harvard you can feel the lock positively disengage. Gentle left brake and the nose moves to port: a quick glance over my right shoulder to check the tail is clear. Check temperatures and pressures (T's and P's) with the shutters full open the needles are sitting nice and steady in the green band.

Keep it weaving, look well ahead. The visibility is not too bad. The canopy is open so I can lean to each side to see down the side of the nose. Feeling the warmth of the exhaust as I do so.

Reaching the holding point I turn the aircraft into wind. About 10 knots, slightly from the right. Not a problem but worth considering in all taildraggers. Cross winds can be a problem in all aircraft but in a taildragger the direction can either help or hinder. Taildraggers tend to swing in opposite directions on take off and landing (except the Me109 which I believe on landing makes its own mind up on the day!). The direction in which the propeller turns dictates the direction of swing and in the case of the Mustang prop right (as viewed by the pilot) so the swing on take off is to the left. The

The class geometric shape of the P-51D is shown to advantage in this view of the N51RR

N51RR was rebuilt by Ron Runyan and completed by Fighter Rebuilders at Chino in California.

weather cocking effect of a cross wind can therefore help to keep you straight, especially in the early stages. On landing as the tail comes down the gyroscopic effect of the propeller will cause a swing in the opposite direction. So a landing, in theory, with a slight cross wind component can also help. Very often you have little choice but it is nice to know if the crosswind is going to gain you an advantage. I prefer 10 knots down the runway. In the Sea Fury, if a cross wind from the left is more than 15 knots for landing Norman starts to lose interest (a Centaurus engine rotates in the opposite direction to the Merlin!) Well it's OK for the take-off. I'll worry about the landing later!

T's and P's. fuel; pressure, suction and hydraulics all good. 1300RPM set. Prop lever fully forward. Clear behind, feet on brakes, canopy closed, stick back. Magnetos dead cut check. OK. Throttle opened slowly to 30 inches boost. Noise levels rising, tail's moving around but still firmly on the ground. Back on the RPM lever, hand still covering the throttle in case I need to chop the power. RPM drops to 1800 RPM. Control forward again, hand back on throttle, RPM recovers.

Constant monitoring, T's and P's, look outside to make sure we are not moving. Throttle forward to 35 inches. Tail noticeably higher but still on the ground.

Mag switches are on the right so I have to hold the stick with my knees, I don't want to move my left hand too far from the throttle. If

it was to begin to nose over I wouldn't have time to change hands on the stick. Another good reason for having some switches in their original place as the magneto switches were on the left lower instrument panel., only a few inches away from the throttle. Left mag off, 50RPM drop, on again, RPM recovers. Right mag off 70RPM drop, on again, RPM recovers. All very smooth, more important than the actual drop to a point. T's and P's OK.

Back with the throttle to 28 inches, a bit quieter now. Supercharger switch from auto to high blower. RPM drops, light comes on on the centralised warning panel. Back to auto (selects low-blower automatically at low altitude). Light out and RPM increases again. Slowly back on the throttle, all the way to idle. Alternator warning light back on, charge rate was good throughout. Idle RPM OK. Throttle back up to 1300. Canopy open again. Pre take off checks using my using my standard left to right sweep are now complete.

Call ready for departure. The lady in the tower replies with a clearance to take off, reminds me of the wind and wishes me luck!.

On to the runway, tail wheel lock in. I know it's not a separate item but a good idea to check because the next aircraft may have a lockable tailwheel and that can be embarrassing to forget!

Brakes off, slowly up on the power. Aircraft's moving nicely in a straight line, can't see a thing directly in front. 61 inches of boost available,

should only need 40-45 at this weight. Aircraft accelerating, noise increasing, rudder effective....60mph, ease the stick slowly forward...tail starts to rise - any tendency to deviate is easily corrected...80...90...100mph, power at 45 inches now and she feels as though she is ready to fly. Ease the stick back and the runway slips away. Accelerating quickly now; safe rate of climb, lean forward, ease the gear lever out of the gate and back. *Don't* brake- the notes tell you *not* to. 150mph, OK to climb now. T's and P's OK. Gear up, and lights out. Felt the positive clunk. 45 inches, RPM back to 2700, flaps already up. Looking for 170mph. All that happened very quickly! The aircraft and me are both buzzing! 2000 feet, go to 3000 feet for some general handling!

Oil cooler and coolant shutters to AUTO now. Temperatures start to rise slowly but still in the green. Check they stabilize. 3000 feet, accelerate through 200, 250. Keep the power where it is. Good look around. Height OK, position, clear of built-up areas. Got Middletown visual, somewhere to go if I get a problem. Security - Flaps, gear and gyros, T's and P's. Look out. All clear. Winding it up now to 350mph indicated. At 370 I pull gently into a wingover to the right. Over the top nice and steep, speed 150, combat flaps available but not required. (The first 10 degrees can be used up to 400mph and 20 degrees up to 275mph) T's and P's steady in the green. Diving again, wings level, ease the

Continued on Page 22.

Initial Impressions

nose up above the horizon, 250mph, hold it there, stick to the left, rolling easily through the inverted all the way round. Centralise. Wonderful but that will have to do for now. People waiting. Change frequency to Middletown Unicom and a friendly voice I recognise answers. Cleared in for run and break. No traffic.

Pre-joining, power back now to 35 inches, 2400RPM. Shutters to open, T's and P's OK. Over the fence at 350mph, this *is* fun. Back with the power, look and pull round the corner. Speed coming off nicely. 10 degrees of flap, 20 degrees speed below 220 now. Not able to bring the power right back, not good for the engine. Hate to hear Merlins and Griffons popping downwind! No need for it. 30 degrees of flap now, gear lever out of the gate, speeds below 165mph, push it down. Suddenly it feels very stiff. I stop pushing. *Nothing* has moved yet. Lights *still* out. I'm sure the sequence has not started. Leave it for the moment, speeds good...bit more power....hold it at 150mph. Call for an orbit right. Granted. Look out and fly the aircraft. Safe height. Position myself better in the cockpit. Got to get it down and there is no other way. Even the emergency procedure requires the gear lever in the down position! Don't like to force, but it feels very springy in the mid position. Maybe this is normal. Don't know for sure. Manual said don't re-select 'up' if the sequence is not complete. I'm sure *nothing* has moved. I push the picture of fairing doors and undercarriage legs all in the wrong order out of my mind! No choice.

Re-select up. Right, this time, one positive movement. Out of the gate, push gets stiffer but keeps moving this time all the way down. Clunk, clunk, a light for each main leg and one for the tailwheel. I start breathing again! Downwind. Start the gentle continuous descending turn onto finals. Good lookout, 90 degrees to the runway, 40 degrees of flap. Prop gently up to full fine. Feeling calmer now. Speed stable at 130mph. Rate of descent under control. Just like a big Chipmunk!

Lined up, final notch of flap, speed 120, power to maintain it. Gear, RPM, flaps, over the fence back with the power. Trying for a tail down wheel landing. Last few feet.... Feet low on the pedals, off the brakes last speed I see is 100mph. Virtually all the power's off as the wheels touch. *Nice one*. Must be the aeroplane!

Keep it straight, rudder is still working. Very slightly back with the stick. Let the tail come

down on its own. Don't fly it down but don't hold it up so it drops suddenly. Slight swing as the tail gently falls but controllable all the way. Tail is on the ground, tailwheel steering very effective. Only small corrections with rudder pedals and no brake required. The stick is all the way back. Slowing down on its own...plenty of runway left. Feet have automatically moved

up to cover the brakes. Fast taxy speed so I squeeze the brakes very gently. Slow enough to taxy, start weaving. Canopy open. Look out side to side; all clear. Go to the end of the runway, stick forward to unlock the tailwheel turning left onto the parallel to taxiway.

Clear of the runway so I stop the aircraft.

Flaps up. Pitot off, lights off.

Shutters already open.

I can relax a little now, could have done without the gear problem. Not over yet. Decision time. Do I go back to Hamilton.? I decide I'm not going to put the gear back up until it has been checked. The only place to sort it out is on the ground. Telephone Robs. Better to feel an idiot than have it confirmed by getting airborne again before checking the aircraft is OK. The ground crew are there from *Hogan Air* to put the chocks in. Up to 1300RPM. Dead cut check.

All services off. Radio kept on. Up to 1500RPM, Mixture to idle cut off, the propeller slows, gradually to a stop. Suddenly it's all very quiet.

Throttle close.

Mags Off.

Radio Off.

Battery off.

Flaps down.

Hydraulic fairing door release handle Pull. Quick double check around the cockpit in case I have forgotten something. Despite the gear problem I have enjoyed every minute. This is a wonderful aircraft and the dream I had was now realised.

I flew the aircraft a few more times and bit by bit I became used to the gear handle stiffness. Unless you jump from one aircraft to another a subtle difference is hard to spot.

When the aircraft returned to the UK two screws that were supposed to be countersunk were found to be a mushroom head type. Two score marks were discovered where these screws had been fouling the gear lever. It's much easier to move down now, though I suspect some of the problem was incorrect technique!

This story was to give an account of a first flight in a different type. It takes several flights to get totally familiar and that is difficult when it is not your aeroplane and the flying hours are so precious. One cannot do the aircraft justice from just one flight and I have not attempted to do that. If I am lucky enough to hear the personal account of a World War II Mustang pilot of his love of the aircraft I will understand what he means! **WW Norman Lees.**

Editor's Note: Norman Lees is a commercial pilot and has a wide experience of warbird flying both with the Fleet Air Arm Historic Flight on Sea Fury and Firefly amongst others as well as private experience He now flies with Gary Numan as part of the radial pair with two Harvards - a new airshow team for 1992.

An Affair with Lady Jo

Paul Coggan reports on a flight with **Darryl Bond** from Chino in his TF-51D. Photography by **Joe Cupido**

Darryl Bond ready to take to the air in L.J.

The North American TF-51D has always been of special interest to me, particularly with regard to its shape and purpose. It was in February 1990 that I happened upon Darryl Bond who is based at Chino in California with his interesting collection of aircraft including the TF-51D, an SNJ and a T-34 that was then on rebuild. It was during the visit to *Aero Trader* at Chino that I noticed a shiny new blue-nosed Mustang across the other side of the airfield.

There was signs of feverish activity as the Mustang would taxi out, get airborne and disappear over the Chino hills for some 40 minutes before returning. The hills were covered in a layer of snow, which in the early morning and weak sun looked pinkish but spectacular and isolated. After making enquiries at *Aero Trader* I was told that the aircraft belonged to Daryl Bond and that he had been putting quite a few hours on the aircraft following rebuild. I knew that Daryl was a supporter of *Warbirds Worldwide* and it seemed a good idea to approach him and introduce myself.

I was soon to discover that Daryl is a fascinating, warm and generous person totally dedicated to the warbird theme and full of enthusiasm for his newly rebuilt TF-51D. Investigation revealed that Daryl had been after a Mustang for some time before he decided to go for the TF-51D model, that is generally quite rare. After the usual search for a flyable Mustang (there is always a queue of people

waiting to buy available Mustangs) in the usual places Daryl decided that the best way to obtain a Mustang in A1 condition was to have one built. The fuselage for the project was to be found with Piper who had used it to mock up a new design called the *Enforcer* (the *Enforcer* was Piper's effort to secure a contract for a

COIN aircraft: it was unsuccessful) Nevertheless the Mustang fuselage was available to form the basis of a new P-51 aircraft. The wings came from Australia. They were one of approximately 100 sets shipped there - and Daryl tells us they were used for stress testing. They came back into the U.S.A. and ended up the hands of Art Teeters at *Cal Pacific Airmotive* (a full feature on *Cal Pacific* was published in *Warbirds Worldwide* Number 15). The spars were replaced and new ribs were installed; what started out as a new unused wing became even newer in the rebuilding process! The paint job was by Don Copeland of Arizona Aeropainting, Chandler, Arizona. So, this aircraft is virtually a brand new airframe. It is registered N327DB.

It was a cold but bright morning and Daryl had already flown *Lady Jo* twice that day. I could hardly believe my ears as he invited me to fly with him. Though I had flown in several Mustangs before I had never flown in a TF-51D with the luxury of a full set of instruments and access to a control column! After the obligatory safety briefing and general walk around with Daryl I was strapped into the rear seat and settled down to enjoy the flight. The larger canopy certainly gives you more room to move around than the standard P-51D unit and the whole cockpit - obviously because you can see what is going on - is more fighter like than the hole in the standard D. With canopy closed and the intercom on Daryl explained where we were going and began to go through the pre-start

check; Safety belts secure: Landing gear handle DOWN; Battery Master Off; Mags Off: Trim set for take-off;Rudder six degrees right; Aileron 0 degrees; Elevator 2 degrees up. Next stage was to check Controls for free and proper movement; Wing Flap handle full up; Landing Light switch Off; Throttle one inch open;Mixture idle cut-off; Propeller Full Increase;Altimeter set to field elevation; Note manifold pressure reading for engine power check. Fuel tank selector to Main tank LH (the fullest)........ my mind began to wander as Daryl continued to go through the various checks.

With the canopy cranked almost shut we began to move forward toward Chino's main runway.

It was like stepping back in time. I never fail to be totally awestruck with the pulling power of the Mustang. Even taxying by the open hangars people look up, with the ocassional wave to Daryl.

Arriving at the runways end, we turned into wind as Daryl checked the coolant and oil temps, set the mixture to run, put the stick back and began the run up to around 2300rpm. The airframe gently vibrated and hummed. The engine sounded good. JRS had done the engine so I should have expected it to sound perfect! Suction, ammeter, hydraulic pressure, engine temperatures and pressures....Prop check - supercharger, Magneto's. Idle check at 650-700rpm. Apparently 1500rpm or thereabouts provides the best cooling.

With take off approved and my suspicious ATC eye just making sure the approach was clear with a second look, the Mustang moved out for take off. Trim was being set for take off, fuel boost coming ON, gas on take off tank. Daryl looked around for my thumbs up. I checked my harness was locked and gave an extra tight tug on the straps. I like the straps to be tight (but

not to cut off the blood flow!) as it gives you an feel of extra security. Thumbs up and we were off. The kick up the slats acceleration never fails to impress me. My favourite part of the take off is always when the tail comes up; it's as though someone has switched on the lights; you can see what's going on now! Smooth acceleration, I hear the gear coming up and watch Daryl methodiacally do his after take off checks. Checking the power setting for climb to 7000 feet and we are doing about 170mph. Almost immediately we hit some rough air which shakes the airframe and certainly gets my attention. We head off out over the hills, which are covered in snow. It gets cooler as we climb, and the

contrast between deep blue sky (against the usual smog laiden atmosphere that usually surrounds the Los Angeles basin and Chino area) and the snow is stark. More rough air, and as we start to climb toward the cruise I glance at the instruments. Passing 3000 feet already. This of course is a 1990's model Mustang. Beautifually crafted, unlike the basic military aircraft supplied to the 8th Air Force. Imagine what those shuttle missions must have been like. Six hours, eight hours, and then having to

Top RH: Daryl Bond has more power at his fingertips than any secret agent ! **Above;** Lady Jo gets airborne for an evening flight from Chino - The aircraft is flown regularly by Daryl who also owns an SNJ and a T-34 Mentor.

Above: Lady Jo cuts through the Californian skies with ease. **Right:** the cockpit is very much built for ease of operation and to Daryl's very own specification. It is interesting to note that the light grey interior gives a clean, very light feel and the grey instrument panel is kind on the eyes. Nav/Com. fit is on the left hand side of the instrument panel for ease of use. **All photographs on this page by Joe Cupido.**

An Affair with Lady Jo

land (besides the fact that en route the enemy were throwing everything they had got at you) at the other end at a strange location. What *must* it have been like?

We levelled at exactly 7000 feet, and hit another patch of rough air as we headed out over the mountains. Daryl asked if I'd like to do some aerobatics. An answer in the affirmative resulted in a perfectly executed barrell roll followed by a hesitation roll, all smoothly undertaken. The air became rougher which was to be expected over the mountains.

By now it was time to head back to Chino. In a wide sweep which bought us back onto South we headed for the airfield. The mountains looked uninviting and the throb of the Merlin up front was certainly a comfort. It also occurred to me how interesting it must be to ferry one of these machines over the Atlantic. Now I understand about the beat of the engine taking on a whole new meaning - or rather it missing a beat!

With Chino in sight I could see Daryl busy up front getting ready for the landing. Gas was switched to Main tank, and fuel boost to on. As the speed dropped to below 170mph the gear was lowered and the greens checked as we came in for a long, straight in approach. The prop was set to 2700rpm, as Daryl checked all the various temperatures and pressures. I moved myself into a comfortable position and checked that my harness was still locked. Flaps came down to what I estimate was 20 degrees. and as we came onto short finals full flap was applied. Daryl was pretty obviously well practised when it comes to what we used to call greasers in the RAF, for I did not feel the landing, only the rumble of the tyres as they came into contact with the runway. The canopy was cranked open a little and quickly filled with the fumes from the Merlin exhaust.

We were on the ground. As we taxied onto the ramp and Daryl completed his checks, shut the engine down and the whine subsided all was quiet. I don't think Daryl had to ask if I had enjoyed the flight.

The TF-51 is a firm, stable platform and with dual cockpits is an absolute dream to fly in. Fuel capacity is 92 gallons each side - normal take off weight is around 8500lbs. Take off speed is about 100mph and the tail comes up around 1000 feet down the runway and it's airborne at 55 inches manifold pressure, in 2000 to 2500 feet. The fuel consumption is about a gallon a minute and Daryl says to figure for a gallon for every thousand feet of altitude.

John maloney gave Daryl his checkout on type; the FAA required some 25 hours of dual with 20 hours 'as sole manipulator of the controls'. Daryl generally flies the aircraft twice a week plus airshows up and down the west coast. As an example one weekend was spent participating in the gathering of Mustangs at Santa Monica. Aerobatics are performed on a regular basis; just loops, rolls etc. but no spins.

The TF-51 is available for training at $2500.00 per hour for licensed pilots only. You can contact Daryl on 714-627-8551.

The Editor would like to thank Daryl for his hospitality and professionalism - and please note that the figures, temperatures, pressures etc., are quoted from notes made whilst I was in a highly excited state and should not under any circumstances be used as standards for flying in the Mustang! **WW Paul Coggan**

Sizzlin' Liz

Richard Paver

Paul Coggan of *Warbirds Worldwide* faxed me just hours after *Sizzlin Liz* made it's debut (Tico'91) in Titusville, Florida. 'My photographers are very excited and we'd love for you to write an article about your acquisition, restoration and flying experiences with your aircraft'.

I felt like Charles Darwin. I could easily write a book about the evolution of NL351DM, but condensing it into a simple article would be tough, though I'd give it a try.

The Search

To summarize my first twenty years of infatuation with the P-51 - my salary and lifestyle did not elevate quite as fast as the market price of Mustangs. Spouseless and dependantless at the time, my magnificently restored and modified T-34 was the greatest love of my life.

When the U.S. economy went sour in the mid 80's a few Mustangs were looking for new owners to whet their thirsty carbs. I thought,'It's now or never. Sell everything and buy a Mustang'. Everyone, and even I had myself convinced, that I had special telepathic powers when I sold all my stocks and the land I lived on mere hours before the 'Black Monday' stock crash. With luck like this, it can only be the beginning of a great partnership.

Finding someone wanting to sell more than I wanted to buy was the next difficult step. I had been looking for a respectable Mustang for about two years, but most sellers were unrealistic. Although the market was down and the airplanes were only mediocre, the price tags

David Marco details the challenges associated with finding, restoring and eventually flying the North American Mustang!

would have set their owners free - forever.

Most owners obviously felt that pasting on a different paint scheme and adding certain avionics merely to suit their personal likes and needs, made the aircraft better (translates to more expensive), but the truth of the matter is that the aircraft is no better, but more personalized for that owner.

While I was prepared to pay for a good aircraft, I was not going to pay top dollar for a machine that needed to have that new paint peeled off for rebuilding underneath. And I simply couldn't see flying an aircraft with patched skins, new paint, avionics and a good engine, but with hydraulic and coolant systems, for example. The aircraft had to be restored in total or not at all. I switched my plan of attack and began to address the market for a project.

Fighter Enterprises - Glenn Wegman

Glen Wegman of *Fighter Enterprises* in Ft. Lauderdale, Florida, had entered the picture by now as I was fortunate enough to secure his individual talents for refurbishment of my project once located. We stumbled onto a flyable Mustang in Chino, California and Glenn went out the next day. He advised me shortly after that that I'd 'better get out there', and indeed

it looked like the perfect 6-10 month project.

Glenn is one of the most capable engine and airframe minds I've worked with, and he shares my dislike of patch job restorations. He models most of his creations single - handedly, although he has immediate access to a machine shop with incredible capabilities. If Glenn deems it advantageous to sub certain tasks, there is a tremendous pool of talent readily available at the *World Jet* ramp of Ft.Lauderdale Executive Airport where his shop is.

A full range of necessary jigs, and a complete set of factory drawings for the P-51 came in very handy and allowed for a more authentic airframe restoration.

The Aircraft and Restoration

This P-51D, serial number 44-74458/NL351DM, was manufactured by North American Aviation at its California facilities in 1944 and served in the Royal Canadian Air Force.The aircraft was sold to *Trans Florida Aviation*, but was not refurbished before the company disbanded. The aircraft remained in storage for many years and was finally reassembled in 1979 in Chino, California.

Our plans were to rebuild the aircraft with a fresh engine and completely new coolant system.

Since the airframe would be restored, it first had to be disassembled. We opted to disassemble and truck the project to Ft.Lauderdale Executive Airport, home of Glenn Wegmans *Fighter Enterprises*.

As expected, the hull was flyable like most Mustangs, but Glenn found problems from previous 'rebuildings', and the project grew from eight months to 36! Quite frankly it was well worth the wait and since Glenn performed the total restoration almost single - handedly, I am baffled how the project was completed so quickly.

I flew the T-34 to Ft. Lauderdale from my home town of Jacksonville almost every weekend, and did so more to learn about the P-51 than to help reconstruct it.

To summarize the total restoration, Mike Nixon of *Vintage V-12's* located a good core V1650-7 and completed the rebuilding in his beautiful facilities at Tehachape, California.

The three year, 5400 hour restoration includes completely new electrical, hydraulic, coolant radiator(Martin Aircraft) and oxygen systems. All new control systems, including new flaps, ailerons(Art Teeters at *Cal Pacific Airmotive*) and a totally refurbished, modernized cockpit was installed. The extensive metal work including a new scoop and doghouse and new wing stress panels helped to make for a more authentic restoration. A totally rebuilt fuel system and all new glass was installed.

All fittings and lines were nickel or cadmium plated (no chrome) or anodized. All internal skins were refurbished or replaced, epoxy primed and restored with Sterling paint.

The Mustang is a wonderful airframe to restore due to the simplicity of the basic airframe. While there are many extremely complex and difficult components to construct, the basic airframe consists of four fuselage longerons that the engine and tail sections bolt to. The wing attaches to the lower two longerons under the cockpit. With the wing bolted to a rollable jig,

Top Left: *Cockpit of N351DM (Richard Paver)* **Top Right:** *David Marco with the first of many awards for the newly rebuilt Mustang (Eddie Toth).* **Above:** *Ready to go - complete with hard hat (Eddie Toth).*

and with the fuselage jigged, total walkaround access is available - even inside the cockpit area.

Glenn's experience and expertise was fully realized with the outcome of the first flight. While I felt qualified to fly the Mustang, I did not feel it was in the best interest for my first solo flight to be NL351DM's first flight also. Preservation of history, you know!

Don Whittington owner of *World Jet* and P-51 pilot extraordinare had been a tremendous source of practical knowledge during the rebuild and casually took an hour off from Sunday golf to test fly the zinc machine. Don's report after the one hour flight - "It's a fast one."

The rigging was perfect, and all systems and electronics were normal. Other than the propeller governor not limiting the prop RPM properly due to a faulty overhaul, it was factory

perfect - and then some. Quite an accomplishment considering most of the parts on the aircraft had not seen each other for almost three years!

We decided to fly the aircraft for 20 hours before changing the primer coat to a real paint scheme making any necessary adjustments and modification beforehand. My first flight was anti-climatic and casually smooth except for not sleeping,walking on top of puddles and through walls for the next three days. Thanks to the P-51 dual instruction, there were simply no surprises other than the realization that I was alone in my own Mustang - and it was smooth, very smooth.

Don and I, each put 10 hours on NL351DM and I then felt it was time for the 1200 mile flight to Goederich, Ontario for the grand finale exterior finish.

Sizzlin'Liz

The Exterior Finish

Exterior finish in the authentic markings of Maj.Gerald Montgomery (4th Fighter Group, Debden, England) is by John Edwards and Crew at *Sky Harbour Aircraft Refinishing*, Goederich, Ontario. The eight-colour Alumagrip paint scheme includes a base of two primer coats, two coats of base grey, six thin coats of silver and four coats of clear - most coats individually sanded to create a completely smooth exterior.

The colour scheme was chosen primarily due to my personal interest in the Fourth Fighter Group, a hard fighting, hell raisin' group that was all action. Besides, I thought the 'red-noses' were the best looking paint scheme on the Mustangs.

Since my brides name is Liz, I chose Maj.Gerald Montgomery's *Sizzlin Liz* to focus on. I researched Maj. Montgomery's history and contacted as many people that served with him from his crew chief to Donald Blakesley - all indicated that he was a 'great guy'. After all, who wants to model their pride and joy after a pilot who gained no respect?

Throughout the two year decision process,

Jeff Ethell was a tremendous source of knowledge. We gathered as much information as possible on the paint scheme and developed a total package of computer generated graphics to ensure authenticity on the two test models and for the actual aircraft.

I chose *Sky Harbour Aircraft Refinishing* due to their experience with warbirds (over 40 years) and due to their experience with Alumagrip silver and clear coat. Two years of casual discussions with Sandy Wellman and John Edwards, along with the owners of award - winning aircraft painted by them led me to believe it was worth the flight.

When I arrived at Goderich, Ontario, the paint crew was most excited by the condition of the skins. Very little body fill would be necessary and there was no original paint left, only primer coat from the mostly new metal. The cockpit, wheelwells, and insides were completely detailed already, and there was very little, if any, paint stripping to perform. However, over nine hundred ours were spent in the actual meticulous coating process.

Sizzlin' Liz

Sky Harbour works very closely with it's customers, ensuring the desired level of authenticity is met. A warbird refinishing project takes approximately three months allowing many visits from customers.

The aircraft is checked over for any mechanical deficiencies on arrival, masked and chemically stripped of all paint. Meticulous cleaning and detailing of the metal takes place while the maintenance staff remove canopies, cowlings, controls and panels. Removing as many of the aircraft's detachable surfaces as possible obtains the highest quality paint job, but it appeared to me as if it were back in Glenn's shop 12 months ago.

The entire aircraft is completely cleared of surface contamination, then treated with a mild phosphoric acid solution to etch the metal, and with alodine, a corrosion inhibitor. At this stage, the painters go to work and prepare for priming. All areas are masked and any necessary body work is done. Although NL351DM had few, all dents and scratches are filled and a special high build primer is applied to seal and feather out the body work.

Most warbirds will have eight to twelve different colours in their paint scheme. In most cases the colours are especially blended to achieve authenticity, each colour requiring a separate preparation and application. Once the major colour, such as metallic aluminium, is applied and the design has been laid out, with masking tape, the parts are again removed, masked and painted apart from the aircraft.

Any defects in the application are repaired before the next colour is applied. Usually the stencil for such things as registration, squadron markings and exterior lettering are applied toward the end of the process and painted in the appropriate colour. If a caricature or nose art is required, it is hand painted by a local artist at the same time.

When all the colours have been applied, the aircraft is touched up with a brush by hand, to fix any deficiencies in the paint application so far. The entire aircraft is then lightly sanded and a polyurethane clear coat is applied. This is normally done in stages so the project is reasonably manageable by two painters. The clear coat is allowed to cure then sanded to remove the harsh edges from the design. It is then re-clear coated to create a smooth, seamless appearance. The major task of reassembling then begins and can take up to a week.

Flying The P-51 Mustang

During the three year construction period, I talked to all of the Mustang pilots I could rope in. I read all the books and also flew Glenn Wegman's beautiful Harvard as much as I could. I enrolled in *Stallion 51's* flight training programme with Doug Shultz and Lee Lauderback (see page 41), and for a change of pace, I also flew with Lewis Shaw out of Dallas, Texas. Both programmes produced invaluable training and

confidence. The *Stallion 51* syllabus is a must for low time Mustang pilots, allowing a newcomer such as myself to perform manoeuvres in the dual control aircraft which they may never perform on their own. It's years of experience in several hours of dual instruction. I plan to attend recurrent training almost annually - no different than we do with our corporate aircraft.

As for flying the aircraft, I will relate my experiences as a mere 100 hour Mustang pilot. First, I would not recommend 'blasting off' in the Mustang without ample T-6 time and a check out in a dual control P-51. A naturally talented pilot with tail dragger experience could certainly fly the airplane with a good verbal check out - if nothing went wrong! Why risk such a valuable piece of history?

Pre-flight consists of normal airframe checks, along with occasional after cooler and engine coolant levels, oil, hydraulic, and accumulator pressures, oxygen system, if warranted,then two to six minutes of pre-oil (top end lubrication) While pulling the prop through ten blades. Although relatively straight forward, don't just 'kick the tires and light the fire ' in this one.

For a conventional gear airplane, ground handling is absolutely superb with the tail wheel in either steering mode or free swivelling, depending on the fore/aft stick position. With the narrow but long Merlin up front, the visibility is good by comparison.

After the run up, taxi onto the active runway, and make sure the tail wheel is engaged into the steering mode. A gentle but positive rolling power application to between 45" and 55" MP, results is a relatively effortless take off roll, as long as six degrees right rudder trim is set, and the tail is held on the ground until everything stabilizes. If necessary, final power application to 61" MP can be made after raising the tail and stabilized.

Most pilots flying lighter tail draggers are accustomed to raising the tail as soon as possible for better visibility and control. Not SOP in a Mustang. The visibility is adequate, so keep the tail wheel on the pavement for positive control. While we are discussing operational techniques, I should mention that our simplest modification to the standard P-51 airframe added the most to normal operational safety - that of adding a radiator coolant door position indicator. This is simply a mechanical indicator mounted on the cockpit floor attached to monitor door position relative to coolant temperature, establishing 'norms' for that particular aircraft. If a deviation is noted - there's a problem.

Lift - off in the Mustang occurs between 100 and 105 MPH and from here on out it's just another airplane- a very nice one I might add. Conservative flying habits, adequate experience in aircraft with high power/heavy wing loading and an understanding of laminar technology will allow for much of the common sense necessary to operate the Mustang safely.

The Mustang is SOLID!!! It was made to fly fast, and to fight - not to offer a luxurious, user-friendly ride with hands free stability. Even though, it's a joy to fly and the Merlin is Rolls-Royce smooth.

Some characteristics that a low-time Mustang pilot like myself might notice is the constant need to adjust the rudder trim with even minute changes in power, pitch or speed. Also, in level flight, it does not accelerate as rapidly as one might think with the application of significant power. On the other hand, it does not decelerate rapidly either.

The other noticeable feature is the hot cockpit. I found it very comfortable on long flights, but unless you're flying in the upper level cool air - drink lots of fluids.

Now let's talks about RUMOURS. Anyone who is interested in Mustangs, and that includes most people who know what one is, has heard them - "Boy, if you pour the coals to that baby it'll roll right over - even when sitting on the ground!' "You need to have 70% of your body muscle in your right leg. It's almost impossible to hold on the runway during take off. And if you get it airborne, it's difficult to fly, heavy on the controls. There is absolutely no warning before a stall/departure/spin....." And then the rumours get bad from there.

Like any aircraft, given the opportunity it will bite. As indicated before, an adequate knowledge of high powered aircraft and an understanding of laminar technology will squelch these rumours. Yes, and immediate full power application with degree rudder trim at 100mph, full flaps and gear down might ruin your day - but who the heck would EVER do that in such a machine?

While these rumours are still flying, you don't hear them from current owner; pilots. As for stalls, it's no Cherokee, but it's holdable in almost any configuration and thee ARE indications of an approaching stall such as attitude, airframe sounds, harmonics, stick vibration, control feel, etc,etc, that one should be familiar with, but other than practice, I have stayed well within the normal flight envelope. *Stallion 51's* programme really concentrates on this.

Let's address the 'heavy' control/stick forces. The airplane was virtually a perfect design once in production. Control forces were probably designed as much to keep the airplane from being over stressed. Remove the elevator bob weight, make the aileron trim tab servo tab and you've got delightfully light controls - a panicky pilot with an Me109 on his tail might pull the wings off, however. In other words, I am certain that the controls feel just the way they were designed to feel! In general, my 100 hours have been very straight forward and the aircraft has seemingly done everything it can to make me feel comfortable.

I've found it to be a delightful cross-country aircraft for 21 one to three hour 800 mile plus trips. Best altitudes are between 14,000 to

18,000 feet mainly because it is cool, but also due to the efficiency of the low blower. If a 2350 RPM-38" cruise is in order, simply climb until full throttle and lower blower achieves this setting and round off the altitude for safety. If high blower is utilized, better go on up to 24,000 - 35,000 feet for greater cruising efficiency.

At 330mph and 1.1 to1.3 gallons per minute at cruise, it's pretty efficient compared to most modern corporate aircraft - except that it only carries one passenger and limited baggage! But how many corporate types can begin their descent with a four point roll, hit the first notch of flaps at 400mph two miles from the outer marker, inverted, and complete the ILS with an overhead approach as a normal procedure? Trade-offs!

As the economy cycles to a buyers market, keep your eyes open for a good solid project to restore over an extended period. Get plenty of advice from reputable and current Mustang pilots, study the manuals and invest in plenty of dual control from a qualified P-51 instructor. Fly sensible, don't succumb to air show or peer pressures - and go have yourself a very private love affair............WW David Marco.

One Man's Pleasure

The climate at Vermilion Airport at Danville, on the Illinois/Indiana border is changeable. Winter brings significant snow and the summer pleasant dry heat. Vermilion is a small, well run airport with a general aviation base. You can see most things there from a homebuilt to a Mustang. It is of course the latter in which we are interested.

Danville also houses the *Midwest Aviation Museum*, a modest but not insignificant collection of aircraft and memorabilia. The museum is run by Henry 'Butch' Schroeder, who many of you will know is one of the co-founders of *Warbirds Worldwide*. Butch is a rather modest individual, talented in the extreme when it comes to warbirds, their operation and rebuilding.He will probably cringe a little when he reads of our high regard for his work Currently located at Vermilion is a very special Mustang project; one that dates back to 1981 when Butch heard of the aircraft's existence. Already the owner of an ex *Fuerza Aerea Salvadorena* Cavalier F-51D Mk II (N30FF/45-11559), Butch was on the lookout for another aircraft that he could rebuild to a

Paul Coggan details the rebuild of a different Mustang variant - Butch Schroeder's unique F-6D. **Mike VadeBonCoeur** photographs

more North American stock condition.

Bill Myers of St.Louis, Missouri held the key to Butch's dreams, for in his garage (OK we've all *heard* the stories about the aircraft in barns and the machines just kicking around waiting to be discovered - but this *was* genuine!) he held a complete F-6D-25NT. Purchased from Michael Coutches in 1961, the aircraft had a little work performed on it but nothing major, though it was intended the aircraft should become a long term project.

So it was in 1981 that Butch heard about the Mustang and made enquiries. The aircraft was completely stock. It had never been on the civilian register and furthermore it's identity was genuine. Even better, on further investigation, Butch found the aircraft was one from the F-6D serial block. On checking you could see where the camera port had been removed and the area skinned over.

Being the methodical and enthusiastic person that he is Butch gave the matter considerable thought, and purchased the aircraft with the intention of a restoration to 100% stock condition. This was at a time, note, that this practice was not exactly in vogue - Butch was not to know that the 1990s would see an increasing number of operators and restorers rebuilding their aircraft to the factory fresh condition in which they exited the manufacturers.

The Mustang's serial, 44-84786, was visible on the airframe. Research has shown that this is one of 136 aircraft extracted from the P-51D-25NT production block built at the N.A.A. facility at Dallas, Texas, under contract number

Shortly after arrival at Danville is the F-6D serial 44-84786. Work began first on the mainplane. The aircraft had never before been civilianised or appeared on a civil register. The aircraft has since been registered N51BS. Completion? 'Just as long as it takes..' Butch Schroeder Photograph.

One Man's Pleasure

AC-2400, and on factory charge number NA-124. '786 was modified to F-6D-25NT status and delivered to the USAF on 8th June 1945 seeing assignment to a 3rd Air Force unit based at Key Field in Florida.

On the 8th September 1946 the Mustang was reassigned to the 363rd Tactical Recce Squadron of the 69th Tactical Recce. Group and based at Brooks Field, Texas . It served with the same unit at Kelly AFB and Hobbs AFB before being reworked by Air Material Command at Pope AFB where it was redesignated an RF-51D on 18th July 1946. For a short period the Mustang was re-assigned to the 10th Recce Squadron at Pope AFB.

Right: The special camera ports can be seen clearly in this photograph of the F-6D taken in December 1991. Below: Special attention is being paid to authenticity right down to the instrument panel and cockpit layout, paint specifications, stencils and placards.

Finally, on March 25th 1949 it was tagged 'surplus' and despatched to McClellan AFB in California. Apparently the aircraft was recorded as 'scrapped' on 25th November 1949. However, after attempts to smuggle the machine to Israel had failed it was purchased, in the early 1950's by Michael Coutches. For some years the aircraft was sat in Coutches back yard where it was used as a plaything by his children. Enter Bill Myers and eventually Butch Schroeder.

But that is not the most remarkable part of the story. For some ten years later - when many enthusiasts will have forgotten about the F-6D we reported on in the dark days of *Mustang International* (that is another story).

So the aircraft was to be rebuilt stock. Identical, that is (at the risk of labouring the point) to the day it rolled out of the factory in Texas, complete with camera equipment, armour plate, flare chute pistol, fuselage tank and radio equipment stored behind the pilot's

head. I just hope these machines did not have a self destruct mechanism as well, because if it did, you'd better watch out, for I know Butch well enough to say it will be in there too.

The F-6D was moved to Danville from St. Louis in three truck loads. Butch resisted the temptation to rip straight into the machine and start work - he had other projects and N30FF to fly any way. However, Butch decided that the wings should be the first for attention, and this was as good a point as any to start work. Meantime he would use his existing contacts in the warbird field to acquire parts the aircraft was lacking - including armour plate, camera gear (after some hard chasing) and even a set of aircraft covers. Every lead is followed up, checked out and acted upon.

Visits to other Mustang projects - including the *Weeks Air Museum's* rebuild of the only genuine ex RNZAF Mustang (N921, which itself won the coveted *Grand Champion* award at the EAA Annual convention at Oshkosh just a few years

later) and the standards they were working to certainly encouraged Butch in every possible way. A visit to John Dilley's *Fort Wayne Air Service* also served to fire up more enthusiasm and secured a rebuild facility for the aircraft's Merlin.

Time passed by. Butch continued the search and research. Enquiries located a former 363rd FG pilot who declared he could help with colour and paint scheme details. Jeff Ethell's Mustang book *Mustang: A Documentary History* depicts several F-6Ds of the 363rd TRG in 1945/46 and this will serve as a basis for the paint scheme, which has been ratified by ex 363rd pilot Bill Lindsay who visits Danville regularly to help with the project.

The paint scheme will be natural metal fuselage, painted wings, blue and white nose checks and empennage and the nose painted buzz code of the period.

So, work began on the wings. Substantial areas were reskinned and all the formers checked in the usual way and rebuilt. The wings themselves held some interesting souvenirs including some period candy wrappers, and the signatures of what must have been some of the assembly line workers - these were scrawled on the paint in wax crayon.

An interesting lead on camera gear was followed to fruition and parts that were in better condition than some of the originals were swapped, and the spares store expanded. It was at this stage that Butch decided to have the fuselage polished metal. On the whole, the majority of the skins were in good shape with few dents and gouges. A camera port was located on a hulk being rebuilt and Butch grateful accepted the skins for the ports. Another part less to find.

It was about this time that Butch was introduced to Mike VadeBonCoeur, who had been helping Butch on a part time basis on some of his other projects. Mike was not only interested

in warbirds but wanted to become properly qualified as an A&P. He decided school was the only route. After qualifying at the Spartan school he began to work full time for Butch.

Time continued to pass by, and slowly but surely the aircraft began to come together. The wings were completed. The project lay dormant for a time whilst Butch and Mike worked on the T-6, which won the reserve Grand Champion award at Oshkosh in 1990 and gained Mike a *Golden Wrench* award. The North American fever continued to grip the pair.

The latter half of 1991 saw the project advance still further. Butch had sent the centre fuselage section to an experienced sheet metal man to reskin some parts of the fuselage. A new, never before used doghouse and airscoop were added to the project - the fuselage extrusions that needed replacing were replaced, and one the tailcone and fuselage had been bolted together and the empennage put in place Mike began work on the cockpit, systems and rigging.

It had been decided that the Mustang fuselage would not be mated to the wing until it was absolutely necessary; basically to facilitate ease of installation of all the wiring and systems. This was the way that North American had worked the airframes - and *Pioneer Aero* (see page 8) also work this way. Each individual rebuild facility has its preferences - some mate the wing and fuselage as soon as possible. Particular attention to detail has been paid, in the light of their experience with the T-6 project, to cockpit stencils, placards etc. and the accuracy of the colours.

Significantly, the main fuselage fuel tank has been installed - all civilian Mustangs had the tank removed due to the number of problems caused with CofG problems. The tank will not, however, be used. Additionally the radio equipment is also in place.

As this publication went to press the project was moving ahead slowly but in the same way it has for the last ten years - with exceptional attention to detail. As the photographs of the

Top Left: Armour plate behind the pilot's seat, fuselage fuel tank (though it will not be used) and radio equipment have all been installed. Right: Left hand console in the cockpit - flare gun attached to flare chute; elevator and aileron trim wheels are all stock.

cockpit show, an original gunsight has also been installed, and preliminary polishing of the skin had begun as an experiment to see what the finished aircraft will look like. Mike VadeBonCoeur reported that even with a basic polish the airframe came up really well. Who knows what the finished item will look like? If anyone out there flew with the 363rd Tactical Recce. Squadron Butch would very much like to hear from you. He can be contacted at 301 E. Conron, Danville, IL 61832, U.S.A. Tel: (217) 431 2924 (hangar) or (217) 446 1034 (Business)

Preliminary polishing of the airframe has proved to be successful to the point that it will be finally polished, though the mainplane will be sprayed silver: as per factory finish; paint trim will be blue and white checks.

N1051S- 45-11371 - Sunny VIII

Delivered to the Nicaraguan Air Force on 31st May 1958, as GN121, 45-11371 was later recovered by the Maco Sales Financial Corporation on 8th July 1963. It later passed to Joe Binder of Fremont, Ohio and then through a succession of owners including George Sullivan and Peter MacManus (**Above** -by Dick Phillips). Seen at Duxford (**below**) more recently, the aircraft will be the subject of a full feature in a future edition of Warbirds Worldwide

The Frenesi Connection

The powerful roar of a P-51's Merlin engine at high power is always exhilarating. As we climbed toward the wintry morning sun pilot Jimmy Beasley Jr. showed smooth effort on the controls. Gazing out at the dark green wings of this fine looking Mustang called *Frenesi*, I wondered how the respective paths of pilot and plane had crossed. Their story is a bit different. You see, Jimmy is half the age of this legendary fighter plane.

The actual airframe identification is in some dispute. All agree it is a P-51K. The P-51K differed from the D-model in several ways. Apart from the improved radios and the vertical fin modification, the main difference centred on the propeller. The P-51D used the 11foot, 2 inch Hamilton Standard prop, variations of which powered most aircraft of the United States at the time. The P-51K used an 11foot Aeroproducts propeller in an attempt to alleviate some of the heavy reliance on Hamilton Standard. Unfortunately, while the Aeroproducts prop proved to be about 540 pounds lighter than the Hamilton Standard, excessive vibration due to imbalances in it's hollow blades necessitated the curtailing of it's use.

But as a K model, is this airframe actually Serial Number 44-12139 or 44-12852? As 12139 it would be in the middle of the 600 aircraft built as P-51K-10-NT. As 12852 it would be the last of 300 P-51K-15-NT models manufactured, which would also make it an F-6K variant, with the addition of a K-17, K-22 or K-24 cam-

Robert S. DeGroat reports on the restoration and painting of an ex Dominican Air Force Mustang as the 357th FG's **Frenesi**.

era system for aerial reconnaissance. For this report, we will use 44-12852 due to the general consensus of opinion.

This plane was issued a construction number 111-36135, but the early life of 852 is quite hazy. Several things have been established, however. It first shows up as NX66111, when it was bellied in and damaged quite extensively during time trails for the 1946 Thompson Trophy Race held in Cleveland, Ohio. Jack Hardwick obtained the wreck and eventually rebuilt the aircraft in 1954 to dual control for *Intercontinental Airways*. It now held the *Intercontinental* serial number of 5131, and was registered as N90613. B. L. Tractman, president of *Aviation Corporation of America*, bought the aircraft on 15 March 1954. A month later, on 26 April 1954, Tractman sold N90613 to the *Fuerza Aera Dominican* (Dominican Air Force) for $50,000. Here it would have a lasting career as FAD1900.

The FAD Mustangs were fully combat ready aircraft. Aviation author and historian Jeffrey L. Ethell had the singular opportunity to fly with the Dominicans in 1982, when the P-51 was still front-line equipment. (Ethell, an accomplished Mustang pilot, will figure in the story several more times.) While flying with the Dominicans

(in FAD1900 no less), he was impressed with their professionalism and the quality of their maintenance. He found that the crew chief of FAD1900 had worked on this particular airframe for over *twenty years*.

As usual, all good things must come to an end, and so it was with the Dominican P-51s. By 1984, their beloved Mustangs were retired after more than 30 years of useful service. The nine surviving aircraft (including FAD1900) and a substantial spares inventory were put up for bid.

Brian O'Farrell of Miami, Florida was the winner. The aircraft were each overhauled before being dismantled and put into shipping containers. They were finally returned to the United States after a long time away from home.

Warbird owner James E. Beasley, an attorney by trade, was looking to acquire another Mustang, but one that had dual controls. He was hoping to use the dual controls to teach his son Jim, Jr.(or Jimmy), how to fly. With that in mind, he obtained FAD1900 from O'Farrell in 1989.

Jim, Sr. has been around the U.S. airshow circuit a long time along with his P-51D, Serial 44-73029 (N51JB), which he has owned since 1979. It is painted to represent *Bald Eagle* of the

Oshkosh 1991 father and son team in two stunningly marked P-51Ds. Frenesi is an ex Dominican Air Force Mustang having been withdrawn from active service in the early 1980's and later purchased, with several other machines and a large number of spares by Brian O'Farrell of Hialeah, Florida.

The Dominican Air Force team at San Isidro taking apart one of the Mustangs for shipping to the United States. These aircraft had been in service for a record time and the crew chief of FAD1900 had worked on this aircraft for 20 years!

361st Fighter Group, 8th Air Force. An interesting sidelight is the fact that, though JB is part of the registration, all of the owners previous to Jim had those same initials. Indeed a coincidence.

When Jim Sr., acquired FAD1900, it was a long way from being flyable. The wings had been demated, and the tail removed. Obviously, much work had to be done before it would grace the skies again. After some initial work had been accomplished on the airframe, it was shipped by truck in a severe snow storm to John Dilley's facility in Indiana, *Fort Wayne Air Service*. After rebuild, the bare metal Mustang was test flown by John to get it licensed. Jim Sr. put an hour on the aircraft, now registered NL21023, before bringing it home in October 1990.

Home for the moment was *Classic Air Services* of Cape May, New Jersey. It is jointly operated by Jim and partner Jack Shaver. Jack in particular is well versed in P-51s, having flown and maintained them since the late 1960s. It was here that some fine tuning of the plane and it's systems took place while putting approximately 45 hours on the airframe, starting in December 1990.

With this going on, Jimmy had the enviable task of selecting a paint scheme for the new Mustang. He and his dad had first wanted a yellow nose scheme to match *Bald Eagle*, so Jimmy seriously looked at World War II ace Urban Drew's *Detroit Miss*. However, with so many natural metal paint schemes already on the show circuit, he continued to look for something a

little different. As he explained, "I wanted a green plane."

It was not until Jimmy looked through Merle Olmsted's 1971 book *The Yoxford Boys* that he found what he had been searching for. The Mustang he chose was called *Frenesi*. For accurate colours and markings he called aviation historian Jeff Ethell. He not only could provide that information, but how would Jimmy like the original pilot's telephone number? Ethell had interviewed this pilot for the 1981 book he co-authored with Alfred Price called *Target in Berlin*, Mission 250: 6 March 1944. Jimmy eagerly contacted retired USAF General Thomas L. Hayes Jr.

During World War II, then Lt.Col Hayes had already achieved two victories while flying P-40s in the Pacific before arriving in the European Theatre of Operations (ETO). Here he was assigned to the 364th Fighter Squadron of the 357th Fighter Group, 8th Air Force. He would later command the squadron from 8 July 1943 until 14 August 1944. He would finish the war with 8.5 victories in the ETO to add to those two Pacific Theatre tallies.

General Hayes was tremendously honoured that someone would want to paint their P-51 to represent his wartime *Frenesi*. To help ensure accuracy of the markings, he put Jimmy in contact with his original crew chief, Bob Krull. Both sent Jimmy photos of the original fighter, and started a close friendship with the young enthusiast.

The actual markings for the Mustang were

extensive, and as a whole, quite striking. The camouflage was RAF green over grey. Other markings identified the group and squadron: the prop spinner was painted red, yellow, and red in equal widths; a 12 inch red and yellow chequerboard band around the cowling, made up of 6 inch squares, identified the 357th Fighter Group; the 364th Squadron required the code C5; and the individual aircraft letter was N. Invasion stripes were painted on the fuselage and under the wings.

Detail markings specific to the aircraft included 85 mission symbols, not unlike many bomber of the period had. The data plate, which was retained in natural metal, listed the aircraft as a P-51D-5-NA, Serial AAF 44-13318. A name plate in black listed those involved with the Mustang: pilot Lt. Col Thomas L. Hayes: crew chief, S/Sgt Robert L.Krull: assistant crew chief, Sgt. Gene J.Barsalow; and the armourer, Sgt. Fred Keiper. Hayes' victory markings (eight at this time) are shown under the cockpit on the left side, along with the two Pacific victories he had earned earlier in his career.

And there was the name *Frenesi* (which rhymes with Hennessy) on the left hand side of the nose in yellow. It was a reference to the 1942 hit song by Artie Shaw, and the favourite one of Hayes and his wife at the time.

During May 1991, the Mustang was flown to the paint shop of Dan Calderdale, a team mate of Jim Sr. on the *Six of Diamonds* Flight Team, had earlier painted Joe Scogna's P-51 (the former FAD1936) as Capt. Herbert Kolb's *Baby-Duck* of the 353rd Fighter Group, 8th Air Force, and had done a super job. After Jimmy's hard digging for accurate information on the *Frenesi* scheme, it would be up to Dan to bring it to life.

The idea now was to get the plane ready for Oshkosh'91. I had been aware of what was occurring, and wrote to Jim, Sr. about a possible father-and-son photo mission with *Bald Eagle* and *Frenesi*. He graciously consented, but reaffirmed that we get some photos of Jimmy flying *Frenesi* solo. Great! All we needed to know was the opportunity, good weather, and all the participants.

After nearly two months in Dan Calderdale's paint shop, the transformation was complete. Detail photos reveal the extent of Dan's precision. One look at the accuracy of the German battle flags used as victory markings verifies the painstaking efforts. Virtually all of the markings were hand-painted. And although the time frame had been tight, the aircraft was finished on time. Oshkosh was just one week away.

In the meantime, Jimmy had not waited to learn to fly Mustangs in *Frenesi*. He had already soloed *Bald Eagle*, built up about 170 hours in type (with over 300 in the SNJ), and was formation-qualified. Jimmy and his dad flew the two P-51s to Oshkosh.

The show at Oshkosh resulted in *Frenesi* being awarded *Best* P-51. Our photo mission, judging from the pictures, went extremely well. With everyone being formation-qualified, and the T-28 photo pilot being my good friend Pete Knox, who taught formation flying in the military, my job was made much easier. We even tacked on Ed Shipley with his P-51 and Bill Greenwood with his Spitfire Mk9T for good measure.

But the story does not end there. Through General Hayes, Jimmy located the armourer of *Frenesi*, Fred Keiper. Somehow it is not surprising to learn that Fred lives within a couple of *minutes* of the airport where *Frenesi* is kept.! Jimmy called him, then took him for a ride in the fighter, though he would be seeing Fred again soon. (Unfortunately, the final member of the crew, assistant crew chief Gene Barsalow, has passed away.)

Jimmy had been invited to attend the 357th Fighter Group reunion with *Frenesi* at Dobbins AFB, Georgia, over 29 August to 1 September 1991. He picked up Jeff Ethell on the way there, and was looking forward to meeting General Hayes in person.

He had a grand time, getting the opportunity to give General Hayes and Bob Krull each a ride in the fighter. But the pinnacle had to be flying in a 3 ship of Mustangs, all in 357th markings.

Colour Spread overleaf: *Jim Beasley Jr. in Frenesi in company with his father, James E. Beasley in Bald Eagle. (Robert S. DeGroat)*

Photos courtesy Jim Beasley Jr.: **Top:** *Mating fuselage to wings - a tricky job requiring skill and patience!* **Centre:** *This makes it all worthwhile -* **Left to right:** *Crew Chief Bob Krull, Jim Beasley and General Tom Hayes.* **Lower:** *Just prior to paint being applied. Taped off areas are evident in this view taken outside Dan Calderale's paint shop. Jeff Ethell helped with research into the paint scheme. The result is stunning!*

The Frenesi Connection

Richard Peterson was lead, flying Charles Osborn's P-51, painted to resemble Peterson's own Hurry Home Honey. General Chuck Yeager flew left wing in Gary Honbarrier's Glamorous Glen III, with previous owner Connie Bowlin along for the ride. Jimmy flew right wing with General Hayes strapped in the back seat. It was a very special occasion.

Heading home, he let Jeff Ethell get reacquainted with the Mustang he had flown in the Dominican Republic almost ten years before.

The fighter, no longer carrying all that armour plate or armament, flies so much differently now.

I collected my thoughts as Jimmy placed Frenesi into the landing patter at Northeast Philadelphia Airport, home now to both Bald Eagle and Frenesi. The story had come full circle with my ride in the aeroplane, and brings us up to date. Jimmy knows full well the privilege of flying such a historic aircraft as the P-51, and certainly appreciates the special opportunity

and honour of flying with some famous World War II fighter aces. Jimmy, only 24 years old has completed the Pre-Med curriculum at Temple University, and now attends the University of Pennsylvania Medical School. He has impressed many with his friendliness and enthusiasm. Thank to him and his dad, I had the chance to observe a unique story about two present day P-51 pilots. It is examples like this That makes involvement with warbirds so rewarding.

Ex RCAF Mustangs

A large proportion of the civilian Mustangs extant today can be traced back to the Royal Canadian Air Force. **Top** (Dick Phillips) shows N6301T/44-74813 (ex RCAF 9261) which is currently owned by Jack Rodgers of Rockford, Illinois. **Below:** It's that Mustang again! N6356T, seen here as N72FT/44-74494 being raced by Tiger Destefani, Reno late 1970s (Bill Larkins)

Adjusting My Attitude

The gentle vibration from both the Packard V-1650 engine and the airframe, massages the body and mind into a world of it's own. The tranquillity is, however, soon shattered when through my headset I hear Lee's voice giving me my next set of instructions. Quickly I return to the real world of flying as I sit under the rear of the canopy of *Stallion 51 Corporation's* TF-51 Mustang, *Crazy Horse*.

Outside the blue, almost cloudless sky, beckons us to fly higher and higher but the Controlled Airspace for Orlando International Airport places a physical constraint on our activities at this stage. However this does not in any way stop Lee putting the time to good use as he passes on to me some of his vast Mustang flying experience.

I had found myself back in Orlando with some time to spare and on contacting *Stallion 51*, I had found out that they could fit me in for one hour in the Mustang. So that is how it all started: what was to become for me the most enjoyable flight I have ever had in my life and the greatest inspiration to finish the rebuild of my own aircraft.

I had arranged to fly late in the afternoon, but before even sitting in the aircraft I was given a briefing session by Lee. It was then that I started to appreciate even more how well structured and organised my flying detail was going to be.

Derek Macphail swaps his Boeing 757 for a much neater North American TF-51D Mustang and experiences attitude adjustment with **Stallion '51**

Here was a man who had done it all before, but he still was aware that it was my first time. I was going to do this at this point as we left the airfield and this at this point as his finger slid over a map showing me the departure tracks to be flown on leaving Kissimmee.

This was *not* going to be a 'keep the wings level' exercise; he was going to make sure that I was going to be exposed to as much Mustang flying as airspace restrictions and time would allow. He was 'my kind' of instructor! I wanted to fly the Mustang as much as possible...and he was going to let me!

I had mentioned to Lee at the start of the briefing that I thought there were two things he should know. The first was that I had not flown a taildragger for 6 years and the second was that I had never flown aerobatics. My fears subsided as Lee's comforting voice talked me through the routine. Sensing the presence in the background of a friendly pair of hands and feet for the controls, if need ever arose, was also a further comfort. Besides he was not going to let me hurt his airplane...not that I would have of course!

On completion of the briefing it was down to the airfield to meet *Crazy Horse* and carry out a pre-flight inspection of the aircraft. I was shown the rear seat in the cockpit which was to become my 'home' for the next hour. Lee fitted me into the parachute harness and then into the rear seat harness. I now felt like part of the aircraft. I certainly was not going to move during the aerobatic parts of the flight detail. The emergency brief over, Lee then went over the controls in the rear cockpit and there we struck a problem. I could not reach and operate the flap selector lever with my left hand so we contemplated using my right hand to reach over and down the left side of the cockpit. Just possible but not an ideal solution, besides I must have looked like a bowl of spaghetti sitting there in the back with my arms all crossed up!

It was time for a compromise. Lee would do the flap selection for me from the front cockpit. Why the problem? Well I measure in at 6 feet 4 inches tall and 16 stones (224 pounds) and the rear cockpit was not really designed for

All part of the Stallion 51 training programme - Derek Macphail examines the TF-51D on a walk-around pre-flight before getting airborne (Marcus MacLean)

somebody of my healthy size! 'Normal people have no problems' I heard somebody jokingly say.

When we are both happy, Lee sets himself up in the front seat and starts to run through the pre-start checks. As this is going to be a one hour sortie Lee does the checks; however if it was to be part of my Check Out then I would

to taxi like a hardened Mustang pilot zig-zagging (yawing) the aircraft down the taxiway. I am surprised just how easy it is to do even from the rear seat as I enjoy a view that is even more restricted than Lee's. Yes, you do have to look well in front of the aircraft and so plan ahead but it all works well. I even manage to miss another aircraft that is taxiing towards us as we

be expected to know and perform all the checks required. The checks are designed to follow a flow pattern around the cockpit, so 'we' start in the lower left side of the cockpit and work our way around to the right side. The only vital control that is not duplicated in the rear of the cockpit is the undercarriage (gear) selector.

Checks complete, Lee slides the canopy partially closed and shouts 'Clear' while visually checking that nobody is around the front of the aircraft as he is about to start the engine. The ground crew of Pete and Richard Lauderback has meanwhile been satisfying themselves that 'their' Mustang is fit to fly, and it is now safe to start the engine.

The starter motor starts to turn the crankshaft which in turn rotates the Hamilton Standard propeller and slowly I see the blades turn in front of me in a large arc. Then, suddenly they all merge into one large disc as the engine fires into life with it's customary puff of smoke and a mighty roar. I then realise that the engine noise is different! It is not the Merlin Song that I expect to hear when I am watching Mustangs fly by as a spectator, still I can accept it and let those outside appreciate the sound!

No sooner has the engine fired into life when I hear the 'after start checks' being completed by Lee while I follow him through the items. Everything checks out, so it is time to start taxiing as the cooling system for the engine, whilst very effective in flight, does not like prolonged ground running with high ambient temperatures. When clear of the adjacent light aircraft Lee gives me control of the aircraft and I start

taxi along the disused runway at Kissimmee.

Having checked the active runway we crossed it in order to turn left on to another taxiway. This gave me the opportunity to use the steerable tailwheel on the Mustang to it's limit. If I hold the control column fully back I can then turn the tailwheel 6 degrees either side of centre by using the rudder pedals. It is very effective and we negotiate the turn without any problems.

On approaching the holding point for the runway we have to position the aircraft into wind so the control column is pushed forward into the neutral position to unlock the tailwheel steering and the slipstream from the propeller together with rudder is used to position the aircraft as required.

It is 'checks time' again, so the 'before take-off checks' are completed. Among other things we check and cycle the propeller to make sure the constant speed unit will control the propeller blade angle as required. The magnetos are checked to see that there is not an excessive drop in R.P.M. when they are alternately switched off. The temperature and pressures are also checked while the trims are set for take-off. This aircraft requires right rudder trim to be applied to assist in the take - off. All checks complete, then it's time to go flying.

The approach is clear so we taxi out onto the runway and line up on the centre line. Locking the tailwheel, take-off power is set and the noise level starts to increase while the aircraft appears to come alive. We start to accelerate down the runway and at 60 knots raise the tail

of the Mustang off the ground so that we now have a nearly level attitude. My view of the world has suddenly improved by this action. Then with a further increase of speed it is gently back on the control column and we are flying.

Soon after take-off Lee retracts the undercarriage. It is not all show when you see Mustang pilots retracting the undercarriage soon after becoming airborne. The reason is that there is a limiting airspeed at which the undercarriage can be stuck out in the airflow. Do it above this speed and you will mostly likely cause some damage or even shed an undercarriage door or two. This speed for a Mustang can soon be exceeded after take-off if you are not careful as the aircraft accelerates quickly.

We reduce power after take-off once we are cleaned up and then turn left and depart the zone to the West. I try to establish a straight and level attitude firstly by looking outside and then confirming it all on the instruments. To my

surprise this is an aircraft that requires a nose down attitude to fly level while any changes in power setting immediately require a retrim not only of rudder but, sometimes, aileron as well. It handles nicely even if it is heavier on the control column forces than I thought it would be.

Unable to climb any higher due to the controlled airspace above us, Lee makes me experiment with the Mustang to gauge the feel and learn how it responds to my control inputs. We change power settings, slow the aircraft down, see the effects of rudder and propeller at slow speed and of course retrim time and time again. I have flown 21 different types of aircraft but this is the first for me that has required me to use the trims so much to fly the aircraft correctly. Still it makes me aware that my flying must be too easy these days!

We soon manage to climb as we are no longer restrained by the airspace above us. A series of turns are conducted with increasing angles of

Pictures this page: Taxy out for take-off from Kissimmee, the home of Stallion '51s world famous Mustang training school (Marcus MacLean): Main Picture- Doug Schultz in Crazy Horse leads Lee Lauderback in Charles Osborne's N3751D/44-73206 Hurry Home Honey (a colour scheme inspired by the Editor incidentally!)by E. Toth. Above: From Bob DeGroat comes this study of Crazy Horse accompanied by Vlado Lenoch in the Fort Wayne based Moonbeam McSwine (N2151D/44-12473)

bank as the exercise develops. The need to lead with rudder to aid a manoeuvre becomes apparent and how it improves the initial roll rate. Eventually we are doing climbing turns at 110 knots with 20 degrees pitch up attitude. All the time we have good control authority and this leads into the regime of stalls.

The Mustang's speed is further reduced to 80 knots at which speed we run out of trim inputs so to keep the aircraft in balance we are only left with control inputs: no problems so far. There is no stall warning system on the Mustang and only very light aerodynamic buffeting can be sensed through the controls as you approach the stall (clean- no flaps down) at about 70 knots indicated. Recovery is no different from other aircraft but there is a tendency for the left wing to drop at the stall; but this can be picked up with rudder and aileron soon after the recovery is initiated. Too quick and aggressive a recovery and you could produce a secondary stall that is overcome by relaxing the control column back-pressure again.

Further stalls are practiced with full flap, giving a lower stalling speed and then into accelerated stalls in the turn with a higher power setting. Happy with my progress, Lee advises me that we are going to do rolls and barrel rolls. Interesting, I thought, especially as my flying so far had not included aerobatics for various personal reasons. What a great time to learn, so lets go for it! Lee demonstrates the first one and then it is over to me. Nose up pitch of 20 degrees, relax the back-pressure and full aileron in the required direction. Low and behold the world goes around as it is supposed to! First time I have not relaxed the back-pressure sufficiently so we loose a bit of height and as a 'punishment' Lee makes me do it again! He tells me this time to look outside and stop flying the Mustang on instruments, as he had been watching me through his interior rear view mirror. As I said earlier he is always there!

I really start to feel at home doing rolls and I am enjoying every minute of the experience.

Still what better platform could I have for my first aerobatics than a Mustang. The rolls lead naturally into a 1/2 Cuban Eight and my world takes on a new perspective. The Mustang is rolled upside down then the nose is down, the airspeed builds up to 280 knots and then it is back-pressure on the control column as we pass the vertical at 190 knots and over the top at 80 knots.

Then it is right into a loop but this time I come over the top with my wings slightly off the level but no problem as I am 'punished' again by having to do it again. How I enjoy the punishment! Next loop we start but this time we roll off the top rather than complete the whole loop. Speed is back at 120 knots and now it is a roll inverted and pull through the rest of the loop exciting at 300 knots having pulled 4 1/2 G (Your body has an apparent weight of 4 1/2 times it's normal weight). Maintaining the speed we descend to a lower level and experience the effect of speed on all the control surfaces with a greater physical effort being required to displace the surfaces. Then to turn the energy to our benefit we raise the nose of the Mustang to a 45 degree pitch up attitude and carry out a roll in the climb, then levelling off to do 4 point rolls. This is a roll where you start with your wings level then stop momentarily with your wings in the vertical, level again but upside down, and then vertical again before returning to a wings level, right way up attitude.

We were now heading back to Kissimmee when Lee declared that he had seen a 'hostile' target and duly gave me a 'dive bombing demonstration' as we bombarded 'the tent in it's desert surroundings'! On recovering from the attack Lee gave me back *Crazy Horse* and it was low level back to Kissimmee.

Before entering the pattern it was pre-landing checks while looking for other traffic to find out that it was all ours so it was down the runway for a 'run and break' with a 70 degree banked left turn to the downwind leg. As the speed reduced Lee 'popped' the gear down and gave me some flap. The base turn for the run-

way saw 30 degrees of flap being applied and the full landing flap being taken on finals. This was for a touch and go landing.

The landing was to be a 'wheeler' during which time I would keep the tail off the ground and Lee would reselect the flaps to take-off selection. The change in flap selection required me to apply forward control column pressure to keep the tail flying, then it was airborne again for another circuit for a full stop landing this time. The only difference being as the airspeed decays after touch down the tail is gently lowered onto the ground and *gently* the wheelbrakes are applied. I had no desire to be strapped into a Mustang sitting on it's nose in the middle of a runway due to over zealous braking!

Lee taxied the Mustang off the runway then I taxied back to the hangar, continuing to zigzag as required. As we approached the hangar Lee came up with what I consider to be the quotation of the trip. The taxiing speed had slowly been creeping up so I retarded the throttle to idle to let the speed reduce. A little while later Lee asked me to increase the R.P.M. slightly saying 'As a Mustang, not only do you have to look good, BUT you have to sound good!'

In the confines of the hangar area Lee took over control and positioned the Mustang so that it could be placed back in the hangar for the night, but not before he had run his last lot of checks.

I emerged from the rear seat elated and exhausted. It had been the flight of a lifetime for me and we had done so much in that hour. I had found the trip due to the Florida heat a bit draining, but what the heck! I would be back tomorrow given half the chance!

Back home in the cool weather of Scotland I reflect upon my time in *Crazy Horse* and occasionally play the video tape of 'my' sortie. The entire flight is recorded in detail....including the occasional mistakes! So with the help of Lee and his Team I had a flight to remember while 'Adjusting my Attitude'. Thanks Guys. **WW**
Derek Macphail.

Double Trouble two Eastbound

O ver a long period now I have cultivated personal contacts with aerobatic, antique and warbird groups in the United States. For without personal contacts it is not easy to acquire good antique aircraft. It would take a long time to tell the story of our breakthrough into the P-51 scene. Anyway it was finally possible for Max Vogelsang and me to purchase a P-51D. It was *Double Trouble two* that in 1985 took the prize for the best P-51 at Oshkosh. The aircraft had already seen service in Europe during World War II and had served among others also in Italy. I took on responsibility for the organisation and preparations for this venture. During my last visit before the ferry flight with the previous owner Donald Davidson of Nashua, New Hampshire, I attended to the last minute administrative and technical concerns. Among other things we also established an association called *Swiss Warbirds*. The goals of the association are the care and management of such aircraft and to maintain the bond we have with our American friends. The question of the risk involved occupied our thoughts.

My experience with 15 trans-Atlantic flights with single and twin engined aircraft, and my career related flying experience allowed me to judge the risk myself. It demands discipline and no over estimation of one's abilities. Though we had very little experience with the aircraft itself, I was familiar with the different routes, airports, air traffic procedures and rescue services. The weather during the late summer months is suitable for a crossing. A few impor-

Christian Schweizer explains how he and Max Vogelsang ferried a North American P-51D over the Atlantic in 1990.

tant principles are; the trip must be planned so that any emergency landing, ditching or parachute jump can be survived even in the most inhospitable place. Don't allow yourself to be stressed, organise and think through all things that cannot be performed in the air.

On the 17th of August 1990 we travelled to Nashua. The flight over in a comfortable airliner gave us time to study our information again. On the 18th we arrived at the airport in Nashua, finding the aircraft in an annual inspection performed by the FAA. Due to engine problems and final clean up work the aircraft wasn't ready for us. We used this time to arrange and check equipment and for flight planning. We confirmed the date of the 21st of August by the ferry equipment specialist *Aero Fusion* in Bangor, Maine for the installation of short wave radios and LORAN C navigational equipment. On Sunday the 19th we were able to do a test flight with the P-51. Since our check ride in Florida in February 1990, a lot of time had passed and we needed a good refresher. During an IFR test flight the navigation system proved unreliable. A local radio shop had to test and even replace a few of the instruments. The radio compass didn't make a dependable impression either.

especially since the LORAN C coverage up north is worse than the book says it is. Therefore we decided to buy a satellite navigation system. But because of the outbreak of the Gulf War such a system was hard to come by. We found one with a decent delivery date and had it sent to Bangor, where the rest of our equipment had to be installed anyway. On Monday 20th we accustomed ourselves to the different checks and landing performance of the P-51 Mustang. Due to it's systems and weight, it is a demanding aircraft. We managed though because of our experience with other high horsepowered taildraggers. On the morning of the 21st we said goodbye to our friends and headed toward Bangor.

Generally we chose short routes close to airports. Because underwing tanks could have cost us 12 to 15 knots and system security we did not install them. The range of 1000nm without wing tanks was enough for a middle distance leg of 700 nm. It was also important for us to check the aircraft for leaks as often as possible. The two cooling systems and the oil system that all have long lines to the radiators got all our attention at every intermediate landing. With a cruise speed of 480km/h in fantastic

***Top:** N51EA airborne at Duxford for the 1991 Classic Fighter Display with Christian at the controls. Nashua, New Hampshire based Don Davidson was responsible for the rebuild of the aircraft which he acquired from Ray Stutsman. The Mustang originally served with the 355th Fighter Group coded WR-P (Gary Brown Collection).*

VFR weather we reached Bangor after an hours' flight. What we found at *Aero Fusion* did not excite us: lots of aircraft, no equipment, and no personnel to install it. Unfortunately we had to show our nasty side to get the promised equipment. Luckily we were able to install the units ourselves.

After a test flight that same evening we were ready to continue. Because not all Americans take dependability seriously, our global positioning system (GPS) was not on the scheduled flight. After inquiry we were promised that we would receive our equipment the next morning. Because of fog in Bangor the scheduled flight had to land in Boston. We made use of the time by studying aircraft and equipment systems.

The local television and radio networks had also arrived for a live transmission. At 2:00 pm we had our GPS in the cockpit and were finally ready for takeoff. Our first destination was Sept-Iles which lies on the northern shores of the St Lawrence river. During ground time Max serviced the Mustang while I took care of flight planning, customs, and airport fees.

An hour after landing we pushed the throttle forward to take off in the direction of Kuujjuaq on Ungava bay. Our route led over Wabush and Schefferville. Flying along at altitude we enjoyed a picture book view of the Canadian tundra.

Often when we flew over smaller airports and the controllers realized what was flying overhead the identical question was asked 'Confirm you are a P-51?' After affirmation the question was asked 'Can you come back and make a low pass?' Unfortunately we could not always take those wishes into consideration. Especially when we could not illicit reduced landing fees! Shortly before midnight, flying in the twilight we turned into down wind at Kuujjuaq (formerly Fort Chimo). I acknowledged the tower's report of a 25kt side wind with an increased pulse rate. After a happy landing we parked the Mustang in the open, well secured, and took shelter in the only hotel in town.

On the morning of August 22nd, the local weather wasn't too friendly with heavy winds and rain so we entered an instrument flight plan. While Max was busy with fuelling and preflight checks, I was busy changing the GPS receiver power supply. Soon enough we were ready to go, taxiing to the threshold; destina-

tion Iqualit. Iqualit used to be named Frobisher Bay. Recently the Canadian government allowed the names of many towns to be changed to Eskimo language.

The winds by this time had reached 35 to 45 knots, and a take-off from the main runway was too risky. Thus we were able to use an emergency gravel runway directly into the wind. Our course led along the western shore of Ugava Bay, then over the Hudson Straits to Frobisher Bay. The airport at Iqualit is situated at the end of the bay between cliffs characterised by snow and ice. Owing to comm. radio problems we had a longer ground time than planned.

Except for the GPS, the navigation equipment didn't excite us at all. Over longer distances the radio compass became useless. And my doubts about the LORAN C also proved themselves. Only now and then did the overlapping of the signal allow a position fix. On the other hand the GPS exceeded all expectations, so that we navigated primarily through the GPS. After all preparations were finished, our heavily laden Mustang with the unmistakable Rolls Royce-Merlin sound took off in the direction of Greenland.

The sun lay deep in the north west and reminded us that at home in Switzerland it was already well into the night. The days in August at 65 latitude are still 20 hours long. Our route led over Cape Dyer. The last useful airport in Canadian territory. As we crossed the low pressure trough covering the Davis Straits, the storm was whipping up the sea. A wave height of approx. 10 meters would have made an emergency ditching in the water difficult. At such times the eyes continually circle about the engine instruments, and the ears critically check the sound of the purring engine.

Now and then I would call on an airliner so that in case of emergency radio contact would not need to be established. At this stage we tried to contact Greenland by short wave radio. Finally we succeeded and the weather report gave us hope of a spectacular show on the west coast of Greenland. Suddenly we broke out of the thick cloud cover and Greenland lay before us. Just like in a picture book.

Radio contact was made with our destination point Sondrestromfijord. We made it clear that we were leaving cruise altitude and would not be taking the shorted path to the airport. The following thirty minutes are hard to describe, you just had to have been there. Sky and sea clear to the horizon, fjords in the setting sun, and a P-51 under ones backside! The rest dear reader you can imagine yourself.

Approaching the airport on finals our radio gushed forth 'Hey guys can you make a low pass?'. 'No, we can't afford it with your expensive landing fees' was our answer! The result was an acceptable $200 landing fee. As in all the airports we'd been to, a large number of people gathered.

After a thorough post flight check we allowed

ourselves a well earned dinner in the airports restaurant, and let the day's highlights parade by again. The weather briefing in the morning (for the next stage to Iceland) forecast good weather till over the ice crest. From the east coast of Greenland to Iceland lay a low pressure area.

Because the outlook for the next few days was even worse, we chose to take off. We forced ourselves into the rescue suits or emersion suits that the Canadian Armed Forces use for flights over cold water. Not exactly comfortable, but for survival after ditching, indispensable.

Because we wanted to over fly the low pressure area, we adjusted our helmets and checked the amount of oxygen. From sea level to 3000 m we climbed along the massive ice formation of very impressive dimensions.

If Greenland melted, the world's oceans would rise 6m. With GPS we flew past an American radar station. We calculated an average accuracy of up to 30m on the GPS receiver. We soon reached the forecast bad weather zone.

As we flew along at approx 4000m we suddenly encountered icing problems. I immediately requested an altitude of 7500m to enable us to fly over the weather. The high altitude equipped Mustang allowed us to enjoy the sun in a matter of minutes. An hour later we contacted Reykjavik and began our descent. On finals we experienced a rough running engine. One magneto had quit. Due to an Acrobatic course that I had helped lead in Reykjavik, I still had a good contact at *Iceland Air*. So, only a short time later the aircraft was sitting in a service hangar! The spare parts that we had along consisted of a set of sparks plugs and one each of the system's magnetos. During the packing of the magnetos, the previous owner said that he never had any problems with them. We told him that for exactly this reason we were taking them along. And precisely one of these magnetos no longer functioned. With a little less sleep than usual, but with a complete aircraft, we took off on Saturday heading for England. The route led us first along the coast of Iceland, then across the Faroe Islands towards Edinburgh.

On the following Sunday morning the 26th August, we continued our flight under IFR conditions. After scheduling our flight plan and performing our preflight check we had to wait a full hour for takeoff clearance due to overcrowded airways. Soon afterwards though we were rewarded for our patience with sunshine above the clouds.

As the weather got improved the last part of the trip was again possible in VFR. At around three o'clock in the afternoon we landed *Double Trouble two* sedately at it's new home in Basel. For Max and I this experience was a milestone in our lives and links us with the Mustang Double Trouble two forever. It was a real adventure that one has to have experienced to understand. **WW Christian Schweizer**

Colour Spread on Pages 46 and 47 depicts *Erich Gandet's* superb portrait of N51EA over the Swiss Alps during a routine flight from its Swiss base on 11th October 1990. In addition to the Mustang's service with the Mighty Eighth Air Force in World War II it also served with the Swedish Flygvapnet as FvNr26087 and then later on as GN85 with the Nicaraguan Air Force. registered N6160U to the MACO sales Corporation of Chicago, Illinois on 23rd September 1963 it later passed into the ownership of Ray Stutsman of Elkhart, Indiana.

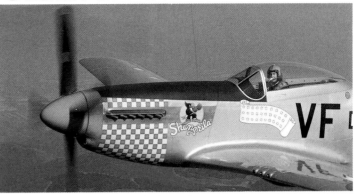

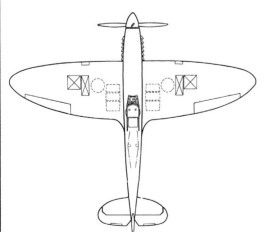

In the laser levelled jig - December 1991 - North American P-51D fuselage. This shows the centre section structure to advantage - note the longerons upper and lower - these are obtained from John Seevers in California. (T.S.A. photograph).

As with most top operations they have to have first class people backing them. No exception to the rule, *Tri-State Aviation Inc.* began as an aerial spraying operation and aircraft maintenance shop in 1974 and continues to provide these services to customers in the Wahpeton, North Dakota area. TSA's founder, Gerald Beck, developed several accessories and specialist kits for agricultural aircraft which he continues to manufacture and market on a national and international basis.

Gerald was born and raised on a farm on the eastern side of North Dakota. He graduated from the University of North Dakota with a degree in Industrial Technology and was 21 when he first went for a ride in an aircraft. He purchased a wrecked aircraft shortly afterwards, rebuilt it and learned how to fly in it.

By now you are probably getting some idea of the sort of person Gerald Beck is. His real interest in warbirds was sparked the day he graduated from college. He was at the local airport saying goodbye to some of his friends when a P-51 Mustang, which was being ferried from Canada into New York, was stopping over due to poor weather. Gerald spent the next few days helping a character named Frank Guzman tinker around the only four place Mustang he had ever seen or heard of. After the weather improved Frank departed and Gerald has never

Paul Coggan talks to **Gerald Beck,** long time warbird enthusiast and the founder and President of Wahpeton based T.S.A.

Gerald Beck, Tri-State Aviation's President hard at work at his desk. (Brian Silcox)

seen him since.

Obviously, this left the warbird seed implanted to sprout nearly fifteen years later. Gerald pur-

chased his first warbird, an F4U-4 (97388) Corsair project, in 1982. With the assistance of Mark Tisler, a certified A & P, he completely disassembled and refurbished every section. The aircraft is expected to fly within the next twelve months.

1983 saw Gerald acquire his first North American type, a twin engined B-25 Mitchell from the H.H. Coffield Estate in Texas. The aircraft was made ferriable to fly it to Wahpeton where it was placed in storage. TSA then added a TBM-3E (53829) - a flyable sprayer from New Brunswick, Canada - to the collection. Due to the inability to find or purchase a set of bomb bay doors during the restoration (a set had recently sold at a *Globe Auction* for a price in excess of $10,000), he determined it advantageous to build his own doors. After acquiring the drawings and utilising 5 extrusions and 7 castings, TSA built 13 sets. The project required the installation of a pattern router and hydro press in the shop, to shape and form the structural parts, plus heat treatment capabilities.

With regard to the North American Mustang, *Tri-State* have made great progress in recent months towards building a Mustang inventory and putting themselves on the worldwide map of serious P-51 parts manufacturers and suppliers. In all, says Gerald '...we have put about 10,000 hours into the development and tool-

Tri-State Aviation Inc.

ing of the P-51 project'.

Following the completion of the TBM bomb-bay doors, with the methods and equipment in place, Gerald determined that sub-assemblies appeared more marketable than individual parts; although individual parts are offered for sale.

In theory, with the original production drawings, a highly skilled staff of tool makers, mass production tooling methods, and machine forming of all parts - variations do not occur in the parts, unlike many of the hand formed items.

Along with choosing this method of parts production/reproduction, over time Beck amassed a microfilm library with production drawings of several World War II aircraft including the F4U, P-40, T-6, B-25, C-45, TBM, PT-17 and of course the P-51 Mustangs. A professional pattern maker now makes the necessary patterns and a certified foundry pours any castings. Although TSA can perform nearly all machining processes in house, the machine shop usually concentrates on building tooling and farms out the repetitious machining jobs to local CNC shops.

The P-51 doghouse materialised as the next logical undertaking due to the purchase of a Mustang project which lacked that assembly. As the project progressed, he encountered the problem of producing the compound contour of the main skin on the doghouse. By forming

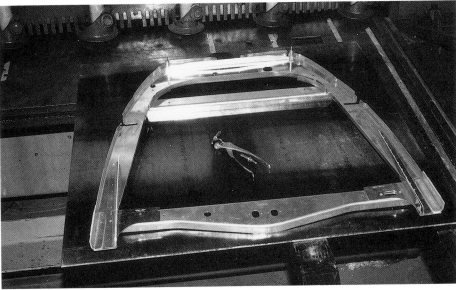

the skins on a wheeling machine, each could differ slightly and take considerable time so he chose to stretch form the main skins and developed the machine and tooling methods to do so.

In order to assure quality parts and assemblies, for all sub-assemblies on the doghouse, Beck again fabricated production quality jigs and assembly fixtures. *Tri-State Aviation* eventually manufactured ten doghouses and the unsold units remain completed in crates, ready for shipment. As with all items, *Tri-State* intends to keep the items it produces in stock, at all

Above: a new component. One of the exciting things about the Tr-State operation is their ability to supply individual parts to other rebuilders. Rear fuselage frame show here before painting (Dick Phillips)

times, to service a growing warbird market.

The fuselage of Gerald's P-51 project came from a salvage yard. Although it did not suffer

Below: One of the new production coolant intake doghouses in stock at Tri-State and ready for shipment to a growing number of warbird rebuilders or an individual requiring a replacement unit (Dick Phillips)

Tri-State Airmotive Inc.

*Top Left: Mustangs parts boxes with some of the smaller components in stock (Dick Phillips) **Top Right:** Another shot of the fuselage jig with a a partly completed Mustang fuselage installed (Dick Phillips). **Below:**One of Tri-State's staff working on the doghouse prototype in October 1989 (Brian Silcox)*

crash damage, extensive handling damage existed along with corrosion of the lower longerons. The fact that this fuselage needed a complete rebuild requiring a jig prompted TSA's next endeavour, the fabrication of complete fuselages from scratch. This project was based on the fact that a survey of the industry revealed that more sets of wings existed than fuselages to mate them to.

Using original production drawings, TSA fabricated tooling for all individual parts and spent approximately 100 hours fabricating the fuselage assembly jig and its attachments. It is built up from a base tooling plate (laser levelled) which allows an ideal reference for all x, y, and z dimensions. The jig was proven by fitting a good, undamaged Mustang fuselage into it; it fit perfectly. Though the shop staff manufacture the majority of parts needed in the fuselage sub-assembly they utilise fuselage longerons supplied by John Seevers of California. Beck does not intend to infringe upon the activities of other rebuilders but rather supply parts and/or subassemblies to any restorer or rebuilder.

After TSA's tool-makers, Glen Geving and Scott Langston, completed the tooling for the P-51 fuselage parts they moved on to the individual tail cone parts. With three Mustang tail cones on the schedule for rebuild, work continues at TSA on an assembly fixture for this.

And what about wings and their components? 'We have the capability to produce almost any part for the mainplane also, but at this point we are not considering doing much with the wings other than certain parts we are hired to do for a specific customer. There seem to be other Mustang components of which there is a shortage, which no one else is pursuing and one of those will be our next endeavour' states Gerald.

With all the work producing the P-51 parts

the common question, 'Are you going to build replica P-51's?' frequently arises and Beck answers with '...a definite no. Our goal is to supply high quality parts and sub-assemblies to warbird rebuilders at a fair cost within a reasonable time frame'.

Aside from the manufacture of parts and sub-assemblies TSA almost certainly qualifies as a rebuilder and restorer. With several quality warbird restorations to their credit, 20,000 square feet of shop,office and storage space, the highly qualified staff at *Tri-State Aviation Inc.* stands ready to rebuild, restore or maintain warbirds for the most discerning of customers.

TRI-STATE
Aviation Inc.

- We have the capability to reproduce your damaged or missing warbird parts - P-51 Mustang included. FAA-PMA.

- Hydra Press work is our speciality - low cost/short runs available.Stretch forming, CNC Machining, Extrusions, Castings all available.

- We have an extensive library of original production drawings

- Contact Gerald Beck with your questions - we will be pleased to quote on your requirements.

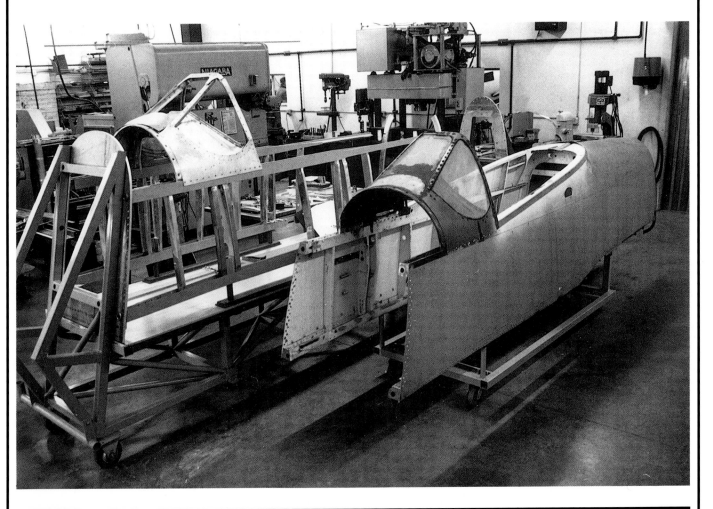

Mustang Flight Safety

F lying a Mustang safely is fundamentally no different than undertaking flight in any other aircraft. You must understand the aircraft capabilities and limitations; you must understand your own capabilities and limitations, and you must understand the effects of weather and terrain in the areas to be flown. Although these requirements may appear to be so basic and straightforward in application that they go without saying, the number of catastrophes experienced with the Mustang would appear to argue otherwise.

To understand the aircraft, one must realise that it represents a device designed with one foot in the 1930s and the other in the 40s; a period of transition from eyeball and notebook design to one of scientific understanding and evaluation. It was also designed and built in a remarkably short period of time, which in some areas demanded sacrifice of performance for producibility. There are always compromises of this kind, but urgency tends to result in a design that leans more toward the manufacturing compromise.

Having related these observations, how do they affect the Mustang? It is obviously aerodynamically clean, but structurally heavy. This produces good speed (compromised by a somewhat high induced drag due to the increased weight) but unimpressive climb capa-

Elmer Ward sums up some important safety points with regard to operating the Mustang and ends with a quiz to test you all!

bility, combined with a tendency to misbehave at the stall. Edgar Schmued's eye produced one of the most pleasing aerodynamic shapes ever seen on an aircraft, but, the level of available stability and control knowledge created a vehicle with a decidedly split personality: ie. an absolute pussy cat most of the time but a flaming dragon when outside it's normal flight envelope.

Stability and control behaviour of the Mustang was further compromised with the change from an Allison to a Merlin engine. Although the original intent was to design an aircraft with near neutral stability, the engine change resulted in instability in all three axes. A narrow chord, three blade propeller was replaced by a heavier broad chord, four blade design. This change was needed for operation at higher altitude but inherently resulted in a greatly increased gyroscopic effect. Additional destabilisation resulted from the deeper fuselage, increased coolant air flow and interference. To increase range a fuselage tank was added that probably

produced the worst aft C.G. problem that ever plagued a production aircraft.

Let me quote from a pilot's manual of the period, 'Fuselage tank full...... the stick forces will reverse when entering a tight turn or attempting a pull-out...In this condition it is practically impossible to trim the aircraft for hands-off level flight.' From *Briefing for P-51 Pilot Instructors*.........'the rudder forces now to decrease... (and) the airplane tends to increase the skid or sideslip 'all by itself', eventually resulting in an unintentional snap roll or entry into a spin,... it is very difficult for a pilot who has always flown a stable airplane to revise his flying technique to properly handle a 'dangerously unstable airplane'. Several steps were taken to regain a semblance of stability. For pitch, the down force on the horizontal stabilizer was increased by a change in angle of attack. Yaw was stabilized by deboosting with the rudder trim tab, and roll was controlled by changing the aileron trim tab to neutral boost. These changes stabilized the aircraft in normal

The Mustang has been in continuous service with either military or civilian warbird operators now for over 50 years. Hour for hour the aircraft has a good safety record, and most experienced pilots agree it is no more difficult to fly than most other warbirds. Here are three Californian ANG Mustangs complete with bombs! **(Bill Larkins)**

flight; ie. stick and rudder forces increase with control surface angle and the aircraft tends to return to normal flight following a disturbance.

The result of these changes is that the Mustang is indeed stable about all three axes; a condition not generally considered acceptable in a fighter aircraft. The ideal fighter is neutrally stable, ie: it neither tends to increase an attitude change by itself nor will it try to recover. For example, a Mustang that is put into a dive when trimmed for level flight will immediately initiate a positive pitching moment if the pilot releases the control column. In fact, to remain in the dive requires continuously increasing force on the stick. A neutrally stable aircraft under the same conditions would show no increase in stick force and, stick-free, would continue the dive with no tendency to recover on it's own.

In it's role as a long range escort, the stability of the Mustang unwittingly became a definite advantage. Inherent stability significantly reduced the workload on the pilot and made it easier to attend to in-cockpit duties without worrying too much about where the aircraft was drifting while looking 'inside'. Few things are more disturbing to the pilot than looking back 'outside' and not recognising the scenery because heading, elevation and roll attitude have all changed arbitrarily.

The effect of stability on combat performance was not as much of a negative factor as one might expect. Typical combat speeds were in the range of 250 to 400 MPH where control forces were manageable (albeit two handed at times). If all else failed there were trim controls, which remained light throughout the operating range of the aircraft.

Probably all of us who fly the Mustang have noted that at speeds above 450 MPH the ailerons and elevator are very heavy and the rudder pedals could be welded in place for all the good they are. However, we spend very little time in this area of the flight envelope and I find that being able to trim out and bore a clean hole in the sky on a long cross-country is a decent trade-off.

Recognising that the Mustang has been rendered stable in controlled flight, what does this mean for the pilot experiencing intentional or unintentional departure from controlled flight? The fixes applied to the Mustang to produce stability in controlled flight do not improve recovery from uncontrolled flight. Except for pitch, the 'stick fixed' stability is unchanged. Once the aircraft departs, the inherent instability greatly increases the time or altitude required to affect recovery. Hence, the Pilot's Manual cautions, 'intentional spins should not be entered below 13,000 feet -in some spin situations you may need that much altitude. Usually, spin recovery can be affected in 1 1/2 to 2 1/2 turns, but not always. The same aircraft may, at another time, take 6 turns while losing 1500 ft.per turn.

In other words, spin recovery is unpredictable

between 1 1/2 and 6 turns. Even here there is a caveat, because should one try any control input other than the 'normal stick neutral (or slightly back) and opposite rudder, it will be necessary to go back to 'normal' and start all over again after having lost considerable altitude! There is some indication that the taller tail on the Cavalier conversions provides improved spin recovery but this factor has not been evaluated by controlled experiment.

What brings on these unfavourable spin recovery characteristics? A combination of things: the relatively sharp leading edge (thought to be necessary for the low drag, laminar flow wing airfoil), loss of aileron prior to the stall, a rudder located well aft of the horizontal stabilizer/elevator panels which leads to blanketing of the rudder, and a long heavy fuselage with a high longitudinal moment of inertia

(includes the broad chord, heavy propeller.)

As with most aircraft, departure from normal flight in a Mustang will usually terminate in a spin. In a Mustang, continued use of power results in a flat spin from which there is no recovery. Therefore, a critical period of time is the interval between initiation of uncontrolled flight and application of corrective control inputs.

The only positive input that are relevant at incipient departure are to neutralise controls and immediately bring back RPM and throttle simultaneously. These activities will minimise the gyroscopic effect of the propeller, reduce drag, and place the pilot in a position to attempt recovery as soon as the aircraft behaviour becomes recognisable.

A spin is readily identifiable because it is a relatively stable rotating manoeuvre. Don't worry about which is spinning, you and the aircraft, or everything else. If the outside is going right, use the right rudder; if it is going left, use the left rudder. As rotation comes to a stop use a little opposite rudder, point the nose down until flying speed is reached, then initiate normal recovery.

Typically, spinning behaviour is induced by an unintentional accelerated stall. Usually this occurs at low altitude, where recovery is questionable at best, and frequently by pilots with low time in the aircraft or who have not explored the flight envelope to any significant degree. If the pilot does not look for departure behaviour, he cannot possibly recognise it, and may inadvertently introduce the wrong control input. For example, if the aircraft nose should start to rotate toward the outside of a turn the pilot may instinctively move the control column aft to pull the nose back in; but if the nose is rotating out due to a stall, this control input will only ensure deeper stall and departure.

In the recent past we have seen two fatal crashes that were apparently brought on by accelerated stalls at low altitude. In one case the pilot rolled at low speed and followed this

The Mustang is a sturdy aircraft and can withstand a fair amount of damage during a crash landing. Nevertheless this a heartbreaking sight though in this case the pilot climbed out and the aircraft is airworthy once more.

manoeuvre with a steep turn into a stall. There appeared to be recovery followed by a second stall at even lower altitude. In the other case a slow pass was followed by a turn and subsequent accelerated stall.

These crashes remind one of Gordon Plaskett's' three rules for flying a Mustang: 1) Don't fly slow, 2) Don't fly slow, 3)Don't fly slow. This may seem like an over simplification but there is certainly a lot of truth in it. How slow is slow? That depends on a combination of the aircraft velocity, weight of the loaded aircraft and the G force of the intended manoeuvre.

Lift of the wing varies by the square of the velocity. This means that lift increases rapidly with increased velocity but it also decreases quadratically. Suppose you are on downwind and after adding flap and lowering gear the airspeed is 150 MPH. If the airspeed decays to 125 MPH or 83% of 150MPH, the lift is reduced to 69%! This rapid decay can easily result in an

accelerated stall on the turn from base to final.

A typical Mustang stalls at about 90MPH. Therefore, at 100MPH it would stall at about 1.2g, at 120MPH 1.5g and at 130MPH, 2.0g. Any manoeuvre undertaken by the pilot will either decrease lift or increase g load. Because it is virtually impossible to fly in the complete absence of manoeuvre, it would seem prudent to consider 130 MPH a minimum flight speed until the aircraft is straight in on final. In turbulence will encounter g loads due to turbulence alone. Because the turn from downwind to base requires more 'outside attention' by the pilot, it is customary to adopt 150 MPH for this manoeuvre.

Another area of the flight regime that can bite is getting slow with the nose high. Deceleration is rapid during a zoom and airspeed decay can creep up on the pilot. About the only indication of speed is the airspeed indicator. Visual references are worthless. Fortunately, the aircraft stability margin is at a lower airspeed when upside down. The clue here is to roll upside down if you find yourself decaying below 150 MPH with the nose up high. No turning, just a clean roll. Roll erect only after the nose is well below the horizon inverted.Knowing that the Mustang has some bad habits and knowing what to do it are not quite the same thing. Of primary importance is maintaining air speed and treating the aircraft to smooth control inputs. Expand the envelope of your experience but do it at altitude. Explore straight ahead stalls followed by departure stalls. Don't get deep into the stall - remember that ailerons are

ineffective, and use the rudder for control. Relaxing stick force and ruddering level should result in recovery. Do these manoeuvres as required to develop a 'feel' for incipient stall-there is a slight burble - a wing drop - decreased stick force - all important perceptions in an unanticipated stall entry.

Smooth control inputs applies not only to stick and rudder but also to the throttle and propeller pitch controls. Everyone has heard stories about the inexperienced pilot that torqued his aircraft right off the runway. In this scenario P factor and torque - both aerodynamic effects - had gotten the better of him. Such an analysis ignores the gyroscopic effect which, in a Mustang as well as many other Warbirds, is considerable.

When throttle and pitch inputs are smooth, the effects of gyroscopic precession are easily managed by the pilot. However, rapid increases in RPM, or manoeuvres at low speed and high RPM, can induce undesirable gyroscopic effects. For a propeller turning clockwise looking forward, a positive pitch (nose up) manoeuvre will cause the aircraft to yaw right and negative pitch (nose down) will cause a yaw effect to the left. In an attempted go-around low speed the gyroscopic effect can be a significant factor when control-liability is minimal but RPM is high because the prop is in flat pitch to obtain the benefit of drag for landing.

Many Mustang pilots use a 2700 RPM setting for the approach. A better compromise is 2400 RPM for it provides adequate power for a go-around and it reduces the gyroscopic effect by

This civilian clad P-51D 44-74850/N2116 became CF-USA. It crashed in October 1975 at Sterling City, Texas. The pilot was killed (Dick Phillips)

20%. Here again the phenomenon is a squared function so that a relatively small change in RPM can have a significant effect on the unwanted gyroscopic moment.

An obvious area of operation at high and low airspeed occurs during take-off. The usual procedure is to use aft stick as the throttle is opened to take-off power. This keeps the steerable tailwheel in good contact with the runway and helps to overcome the tendency to swing left. As the tail is brought up, the nose-down pitching of the propeller induces a gyroscopic turning moment to the right which momentarily appears as a reduced requirement for right rudder. As soon as the take-off pitch attitude is achieved, the gyroscopic effect decays and right rudder must again be increased.

This entire scenario occurs at well below flight airspeed and can be confusing for the inexperienced pilot. Here, as in every other aspect of flying, the primary rule is 'fly the aircraft - don't let it fly you - do what ever you have to do to make the aircraft do what you want it to do - and do it 100% of the time'.

If I have made the Mustang sound like a monster it is only because several of my friends are no longer around. The Mustang can be, and usually is, a great pleasure to fly. It is quick, it responds well, and it tends to make you look better in manoeuvres than you really are. It doesn't seem to take any more attention than a T-6, but it sure attracts more, wherever you go. So keep your airspeed up, your inputs smooth, and have one of the greatest rides an airplane has to offer. **WW Elmer Ward**

Mustang Pilots Quiz

Answer TRUE or FALSE to the following statements - Answers are overleaf. No cheating! Did you get them all right?

1. The Mustang is noted for it's high speed and impressive climb capability.
2. Unlike most fighter aircraft the Mustang is stable about all three axes in formal flight.
3. In a spin, always apply rudder in the direction that the 'outside' appears to be moving.
4. The Mustang is stable both 'stick free' and 'stick fixed'.

5. The fledgling Mustang pilot, regardless of his experience level, should spend time at altitude exploring the flight envelope, especially incipient and accelerated stall.
6. Spins should not be entered below 13,000 ft. agl because recovery is best achieved at that altitude.
7. The lift of a wing varies by the square of the airspeed so small variations in airspeed result in much larger changes in lift.
8. Spin recovery is affected by positioning the stick neutral or slightly aft and applying opposite rudder.
9. Recovery from a flat spin can be made after reducing power and increasing propeller pitch to reduce the gyroscopic moment.
10. In turbulence it is good procedure to

increase landing approach speeds because one effect of turbulence is to increase wing load.
11. The propeller exerts a significant moment to the aircraft when it is pitched or yawed at high engine speeds.
12. Unintentional spins at low altitude are rare because the pilot is usually flying very cautiously when near the ground.
13. The stability margin of a Mustang occurs at a lower speed when inverted.
14. Gyroscopic precession produces a moment perpendicular to the direction of pitch or yaw movement and 90 degree out of phase in the direction of propeller rotation, ie: for clockwise rotation a nose up pitch produces a nose right force.

Formal Conversion Training

Military Pilots train; so do astronauts and airline pilots. They all learn required skills and regularly practice them to proficiency. These people undergo refresher courses in aircraft systems, flight operations and emergency procedures to maintain and enhance these skills. No comparable format exists for warbird pilots. In the U.S., the basic 'single engine land endorsement' on a private pilot's license technically qualifies a person on most single engined warbird types. A Federal Aviation Administration Letter of Authorisation, (if required, can be

> Lee Lauderback and Doug Schultz tell us why there is no alternative to formal conversion training.

earned with little or no formal training) can allow that same private pilot to fly a Mustang, Spitfire or Bearcat.

'Great' , you might say, 'We aren't going to war in these things! After all, this antique ex-fighter

is just another aeroplane, and except for a tail-wheel and a little more torque, what's the big deal?'

Aside from potential litigation, private or regulatory action (we all abhor the threat of increased government oversight). The big deal is that these are not your average general

Below: Robb Satterfield was a well known and respected Mustang pilot and a proponent of continuation training in all types of aircraft. Robb maintained he was never too humble to learn anything - each flight was a new experience. Seen here in Miss Torque N7722C/44-73420 (Alan Gruening)1986.

Mustang Pilots Quiz Answers

1. FALSE. For it's level of power the speed capability of the Mustang was unmatched but the climb rate was 14% less than the Spitfire, 16% less than the Bf109G
2. TRUE
3. TRUE
4. FALSE Mustang 'stick free' stability was achieved by aerodynamic devices that did not correct the stick fixed instability.
5. TRUE
6. FALSE. Spins should not be entered below 13,000ft. because recovery is indeterminate between 1-1/2 and 6 turns.
7. TRUE
8. FALSE. The first control input must minimise power and increase pitch of the propeller to reduce the gyroscopic effect and decrease drag. The apply the aerodynamic control inputs.
9. FALSE. According to the handbook there is no recovery from a fully developed flat spin.
10. TRUE
11. TRUE
12. FALSE. Most Mustang fatalities have occurred at low altitudes and in the landing pattern.
13. TRUE
14. TRUE

aviation aircraft, they are sophisticated weapons delivery platforms designed for combat. These machines don't care that most warbird enthusiasts are not fighter pilots. They don't know that we're going airshow flying and not out trading shots with Messerschmitts. Every time they fly they go to war with the same virtues and the same vices that they had in the 40s. They were and are still among the most exhilarating aircraft to fly, and if abused or disrespected, they can also be among the most treacherous and unforgiving.

Have You Stalled Yours?

After nearly five years of operating our TF-51 Mustang *Crazy Horse*, we are continually amazed at the number of experienced Mustang pilots who have never intentionally stalled their aircraft, who have never flown them upside down, who fly them considerable distances in varying weather conditions without instrument ratings or have never simulated (or even thought about) an engine failure after takeoff. They invest huge sums of money in the aircraft, insurance premiums, restoration and maintenance, new avionics, tools, flight gear, spares and hangar facilities, yet will climb into their aircraft without the benefit of formal training. All the

time thinking, 'Hell I've got 4000 hours, if I can start this thing, take off and fly around a little, maybe do a roll or two and get it back on the ground - no problem!' So, you go through the operating manual, discuss some do's and dont's with other 'experienced' 51 drivers, crank her up and you're off. Right?

Several years back, we received a call from someone who announced that he'd just purchased a Mustang and had ground - looped it during his first takeoff, resulting in considerable damage and expensive repair. During his subsequent training with us in Florida, he discovered many false impressions about the aeroplane, flight procedures, systems operation and especially piloting technique. Practicing his field work, prior to that eventful first take off attempt, to proficiency would likely have saved him considerable anguish and expense, and paid dividends of more enjoyable flying generated through increased general competence. Another new Mustang owner flew his twin turbo to Kissimmee intending to fly a maximum of five hours with us in the TF-51 (5 hours were all his insurance agent required). Poor weather and lack of time prevented any training. However, after meeting us, observing our operation and praising our program, he affirmed his intention to return within a few weeks and 'do it right' by completing our entire conversion syllabus. Ten days later, when contacted for scheduling he announced that he was already 'trained'.

It seems that after a 'few hours' of ground school he sat in the jump seat of his Mustang for two flights while observing another pilot fly various stalls, manoeuvres, landings, etc. That, and a few uneventful solo flights was that.

Ironically, this is probably more preparation than most civilian Mustang pilots had for their first flight. Even fighter pilot trainees during WWII (until the appearance of the TP and TF conversion at the war's end) logged their first minutes of P-51 time in the front and only seat. 'Acceptable attrition' was planned for and expected, and conversion training losses were not uncommon. Today, 'attrition' is not replaced by new production, and losses, though sadly expected, are not 'acceptable'. Our ever increasing exposure to litigation, let alone the loss of our lives and those of our crew or passengers, put just as much of a premium on pilot proficiency as ever. In wartime, the mission was to do the job and get home safely. Today, the mission is to have fun and still get home safely.

Most of us are acutely aware of what seems like a rash of stall-related Mustang accidents over the past two years. This has added considerable fuel to the aeroplanes 'reputation' for little or no stall warning, abrupt and radical stall departure, and unpredictable spin dynamics. The six most recent incidents occurred within two general flight regimes; slow speed in the traffic pattern and high speed manoeuvring at low altitude. They involved predominantly experienced pilots who unintentionally stalled their aircraft and not only allowed them to depart from controlled flight but aggravated the situations by keeping the aeroplane loaded up ie. maintaining back-up pressure on the stick and not releasing (unloading) that pressure - to allow the aeroplane to accelerate just enough for recovery. How long before coming to grief had each of these pilots gone without performing an intentional one-G stall or progressive stall and recovery?

Every six months we contract with the U.S. Government to conduct qualitative evaluation flights in the TF-51 with graduating students at the *Naval Test Pilot School*, Patuxent River, MD. With few exceptions, immediately after sampling the airframe and mechanical characteristics and basic handling qualities during the initial climbout, each student performs one or more one-G wings level stalls, and one and one half to three-G accelerated stalls in both clean and landing configurations. Only then are the main body of performance oriented manoeuvres (high-G turns, aerobatics, simulated weapons delivery and air combat manoeuverings) attempted. Before returning to base for landings, the Mustang's approach turn stall characteristics are experienced.

It should be noted that student test pilots bring a background of highly successful operational experience to their courses of study and add hundreds of flights in sometimes dozens of different aircraft before graduation and subsequent participation in formal test programmes. In over 200 flights (considered part of their official course curriculum) that we have shared with student and instructor test pilots, not one has failed to unload the aircraft as the initial recovery response to a stall or progressive stall condition. Is there a universal truth

buffet.

If the Mustang exhibited no stall warning, then no pre-stall aerodynamic buffet would be in evidence and our trainees could not maintain in excess of fifty degree angle of bank turns and turn reversals in sustained buffet as they seem to do with regularity. This drill is a real eye - opener, and like many other choreographed manoeuvres demonstrated and practiced during quality formal training, teaches us to be

here? (Read YES!)

Our formal Mustang conversion training programme consists of nine plus or minus flights depending upon trainee experience and his or her progress to proficiency. The first myth about the Mustang that we expose is that of stall warning. Even experienced test pilots stub their toes on this one, proclaiming that the Mustang has 'no stall warning', a condition usually defined in terms of flight control responses and the frequency and speed range of aerodynamic

receptive to what the aeroplane is telling us. Recovery from loss of controlled flight is a principle focus in our training syllabus. We begin with entry into and recoveries from basic

*All the Mustangs illustrated on **pages 58 and 59** are no longer extant, in each case the crash killed the pilot and passengers. **Page 58** shows CF-USA, Above Mustang Pilot's Club N5747 (referred to in Airworthy Mustangs in Europe on Page 68) and below is N51JW/45-11546 which was destroyed at Reno in September 1983 killing its owner and his wife.*

Formal Conversion Training

clean stalls on the first flights and progress to accelerated stalls, full departures from controlled flights and recoveries from the modest to high - amplitude unusual attitudes. On the last flight we recover from high-G accelerated stalls, vertical departures, approach turn stalls, post-stall gyrations from 'blown' overhead aerobatic manoeuvres and fully-developed spins. Our objective with stall and progressive loss of control training as with our collateral focus on aircraft systems, critical-action procedures, aerobatics energy manoeuvrability, simulated air-to-ground weapons delivery and air combat manoeuvring, and multi-situational takeoffs, landings and go arounds, is to produce a pilot who has experienced every vice and virtue that the Mustang has to offer.

'Hold on a minute', you might say 'All I want to do in my 51 is take off, do some basic aerobatics, join my buddies at a few airshows and fly home. What's the point of all this military stuff?' Earlier this year, a prospective Mustang owner enquired about our training programme and expressed reservations about our format. He suggested that not everyone who came to us for training aspired to become a fighter pilot and questioned his need of exposure to certain high performance and loss of control, manoeuvres.

As a highly successful competitive driver and builder of world class racing cars, his quite reasonable rationale was that he had no intention of flying the Mustang like a fighter and shouldn't require a fighter pilot's skills to be safe and competent in his aeroplane, much as we shouldn't need professional driver skills to cruise, but not race a Formula One car. Thus pre-disposed to a little healthy scepticism, he nevertheless plunged into the course and emerged from it with a completely changed attitude, becoming in the process one of the more vocal advocates of our training programme. He learned that the Mustang is a fighter, that it's design and function were optimized to the fighters role, and that well below 450 kts and 8 G's the Mustang performs best and safest when flown like a fighter.

Military and competitive aerobatic pilots are especially aware of this analogy. They become so familiar with flying to and beyond the performance limits of their aircraft that 'normal' flight becomes totally straightforward. And that when (not if)something goes wrong, particularly something unintentional, (not unanticipated) that transcends normal operating dynamics, they immediately fall back on their reservoir of

experience generated from exposure to every significant aircraft performance characteristic. Because they have seen and practiced it all, they are able to recognise a problem or crisis at it's onset and are prepared to respond effectively.

The old fighter pilot's refrain, *You fight like you train*', had direct merit in the warbird environment. If you never stall the aeroplane, how will you recognise the onset of an inadvertent stall (due to your distraction in the landing pattern) much less the stall itself, and how will you decisively respond, especially at low altitude? If you've never pulled the aeroplane into departure during a level high-G turn, will you recognise the clipped flash of airframe buffet

(because you pulled too hard in the 'break' to land after your dazzling airshow strafing passes) in time to unload before you snap inverted, and what will you do if you do go inverted, pointing at the ground? If you've never seen a Mustang spin, how would you determine that you had actually entered a spin (you flew into a cloud during an aerobatic manoeuvre, became disoriented, and suddenly you pop out VFR with the world turning around), or, conversely, that you were not in a spin? How would you initiate recovery? What feedback would you have that your recovery inputs were taking effect? How will you determine that enough altitude remains for recovery? The best defence against potential trouble is to meet it or simulate it first on your own terms with plenty of room to get acquainted.

We encourage our graduates to practice much of what they have done during training; to stay proficient with aircraft systems and procedures, to spare nothing in the maintenance of their aircraft, to practice every airshow manoeuvre at altitude before bringing it down to the crowd, and to remain receptive to better and safer ways of conducting every facet of operation.

Should they never again fly into a progressive spin or attempt a tailslide or overhead reversal in their Mustangs, the knowledge and confidence gained in performing these and other practiced manoeuvres during training will enhance their general proficiency, promote their safety and that of those who fly with them and make everyday flying more fun.

Every warbird pilot, whether new to an aeroplane or with hundreds of hours in type, can benefit in often surprising ways from formal conversion and recurrent training. Alternatives considered, there is simply no substitute.
WW Doug Schultz and Lee Lauderback.

Editors Note: There have been comments in some quarters that *Warbirds Worldwide* gives excessive coverage to *Stallion* 51, perhaps because they advertise with us. As a point of policy we firmly back any reputable training programme that will improve safety factors and prolong the lives of our members and their aircraft. As a matter of fact a number of graduates of the course have submitted totally unsolicited reports to us on the value and relevance of the programme. Doug Schultz and Lee Lauderback and the entire support staff at *Stallion* 51 should be congratulated on their foresight, professionalism and above all their dedication to setting high standards of training to only the most professional standard. Doug and Lee were asked by the Editor to submit the above and did so despite a busy schedule. To all at *Stallion* 51 -our sincere thanks. **Paul Coggan**

There is some indication that the taller tail on the Cavalier conversions provides improved spin recovery but this factor has not been evaluated by controlled experiment (see Elmer Ward's article on Mustang Flight Safety). Here is Stallion 51's Cavalier tailed TF-51D (Brian Silcox)

Kiwi Mustang

Trevor T. Bland, President of **New Zealand Warbirds** tells of a dream come true and of some down to earth experiences whilst flying the Mustang

It all started in 1950 when as a schoolboy I watched the beautiful P-51Ds operated by the Royal New Zealand Air Force Territorial Squadrons regularly fly over my hometown of Wellington. I guess I just fell in love with this thoroughbred at an early age when most teenage males are preoccupied with the opposite sex.

I had my first close encounter with the Mustang when as a cadet in the Air Training Corps, I was selected to undergo basic technical training with No.2 Wellington TAF Squadron based than at RNZAF Base Ohakea. I had some eighteen months in *Hog Heaven*, fuelling and oiling (and cleaning) the Mustangs, all the while envying the young university students who were actually being paid to fly the mighty Mustangs on the weekends.

After that came some thirty five years of flying everything from the T-6 Harvard to the B747-200 series Jumbo, but alas never to fly the love of my life-the North American P-51D. After several aborted trips to the USA to try to buy a ride, I had virtually given up all hope of ever flying the Mustang. Then I heard a rumour that Tim Wallis of *Alpine Deergroup* was negotiating to purchase a P-51 from *Fort Wayne Air Services* to be imported and operated in New Zealand. I wrote to Tim, offering some dual in my T6 Harvard ZK-WAR and heard nothing for months. Out of the blue I had a phone call from Tim one Saturday morning asking if I would be interested in flying the Mustang for him until he himself could convert onto the machine. When I came down to earth I tried hard to contain my enthusiasm and to converse purposefully with Tim, hoping that he would not change his mind.

Waiting for the arrival of the P-51 from the USA must have raised my blood pressure, as many fellow aviators kept telling me how poorly I looked and perhaps they should offer their services in my place. However the longed for date finally arrived and I was present at RNZAF Base Wigram in Christchurch when N763MD was

Top: Trevor Bland taxies out to display ZK-TAF at Wanaka in 1990 - one of the most spirited Mustang displays I've ever seen (Paul Coggan). Centre - ZK-TAF at Paraparaumu, 2nd March 1985. It was here that Trevor flew 'TAF on his first public display. (Lyndon Knowles). Bottom: Over the trees at Wanaka (Paul Coggan).

Kiwi Mustang

uncrated. The reassembly commenced under the watchful eye of John Dilley, who had come out to New Zealand to test fly the Mustang for Tim. Alpine's chief engineer, Ray Mulqueen, ably assisted by RNZAF engineers had N763MD ready to fly in record time. John test flew the aircraft and pronounced the Mustang 100% OK. John flew several hours off the aircraft before handing over the Mustang. I was almost beside myself waiting for the opportunity to get my hands on an aircraft I had dreamed about flying for so many years.

After a short back seat ride with John, I was let loose on my own. Having cranked up the mighty Merlin, I taxied out for a departure from the grass vector at Wigram. John had suggested some high speed taxy runs before flying the aircraft, but with some 3000 hours on T-6s, I found the Mustang very stable and easy to control on the ground.

My first take off was a rather cautious affair, as I had never flown a high performance piston engine fighter. With adequate room for the take-off, I set only 55" of boost instead of the normal rated t/o of 61". Even at this power setting, the acceleration was impressive and the torque effect quite marked.

Having tucked the gear away, I headed off to the RNZAF training area and revelled in the han-

However these pleasures were mixed with some concerns. Operating the Mustang over New Zealand's varied terrain and in rapidly changing weather patterns, has raised the adrenaline level on occasions. Placing total reliance on that 12 piece orchestra whilst flying a high profile irreplaceable masterpiece over some of the most inhospitable country found anywhere in the world is certainly cause for concern. ZK-TAF is equipped for full IFR, but wherever possible, it is operated strictly VFR. However, there have been occasions when I have been thankful for all that modern gear.

Operating into Wanaka in the middle of the Southern Alps was an experience in itself. Wanaka is the home of Tim Wallis and the *Alpine Deergroup* and in 1985 the airfield consisted of a very short, rocky grass field with about 300m of seal. With just a few hours on type, it caused the odd cardiac flutter trying to put the Mustang down on that 300m in 20-30 kts crosswind. I was thankful for many hours on T-6s operating in similar conditions.

My first public display was at an airfield called Paraparamu, just north of Wellington. I had amassed 1 hour 30 minutes on type and I adopted a very cautious approach to the task. However, after arriving late for the briefing, having circumnavigated some foul weather en

I rolled into a left turn in front of the crowd and eased the aircraft into a climb. At that stage there was a loud bang and all hell let loose. I remembered a sharp crack on the back of my bone dome that left me somewhat dazed. My first thought was structural failure and my immediate concern was how would I tell Tim. The Mustang was however, still flying and I was not yet in Heaven (or elsewhere). I lay *prone* on the cockpit floor, looking up through the canopy, as I gathered my wits. The seat, which tilts forward to allow access to the jump seat, had collapsed rearward with considerable force and I was still strapped firmly in the seat.

After extricating myself I could not raise the seat, so was faced with the prospect of landing the P51 in some 20kts crosswind, on a short runway, whilst balancing on the front of the seat, in front of a large crowd of aviation enthusiasts. I began to wonder why I had ever taken up flying!

Fortunately, both the aircraft and myself landed without further incident, but my ticker was working overtime for some time and many post flight ales.

In a flying career that now spans some forty years, I have been lucky enough to display many different types, such as T-6, Harvard, DH82, DHC1, Vampire, Venom, B12 Canberra,

dling qualities of the P-51. It was all that I had expected and I would have been happy to loop and roll around the Canterbury Plains forever.

Thanks to Tim and his team at *Alpine* I have had the privilege of flying the Mustang - now registered ZK-TAF - many times over the past six years and have thoroughly enjoyed displaying the aircraft at many venues.

route, I found I was first up and 'please get airborne some five minutes ago'. Having not been long on the ground, the pre-flight was somewhat hurried and I cranked the Merlin up and leapt into my display. All went well until my final high speed pass, which should have culminated in a victory roll. I was blatting across the airfield at around 380kts IAS and about 50'AGL, when

A-4K Skyhawk, Gloster Javelin and F6 Hunter, I still get the greatest thrill each time I walk out to that waiting thoroughbred; taking in the sleek purposeful lines and cranking up that beautiful Merlin and putting the Mustang through it's paces. I am grateful to be one of the privileged few. **WW Trevor T. Bland** (President) N.Z. *Warbirds Assn.*

Born from the Mustang: Flying *Stiletto*

There has always been a certain air of mystery surrounding *Stiletto*. We are told (by experts who had never flown it) it was a dangerous airplane, and that we should not attempt to fly it, much less race it. Of course when we bought the airplane we had no intention of racing it; we are in the sales business, and unlimited air racing, quite frankly, is much too rich for our blood. We did have, however, every intention of flying *Stiletto*.

As Reno drew closer though, we had some tough decisions to make. We sat down and discussed from a business stand point, the possibility of racing at Reno. We knew what the rumours about the airplane were, and decided if we didn't sell it before Reno, the best and really only way to market it, would be to race at Reno.

The people who had displayed interest in *Stiletto* kept coming back to the old rumours and expressed concern about their ability to fly it (and of course flying meant racing). So we figured if nothing else, people could see the airplane flown by rookies, and raced by a rookie.

Stiletto is a modified North American P-51D. The water and oil radiators located in the belly scoop were removed, and new radiators were relocated internally in the wings. The wings have been clipped 8 feet for a total wingspan of 29 feet. The flap travel is limited to 30 degrees, the cockpit has been moved aft 20 inches. The cockpit is a new design, optimized for racing, incorporating automated systems controlled by and monitored by a small com-

Scott A. Sherman of Sherman Aircraft Sales scotches the myths surrounding the performance and handling of Stiletto - Unlimited Air Racing P-51.

puter. Radiator spray bar water is utilized to aid in cooling on the ground and during high power flight. Spray bar water is carried in the left main wing tank, fuel is carried in the right wing, and ADI is carried in a fuselage tank aft of the pilot. It is also equipped with a windshield gas squirter to clear an oily windshield. This is also actuated by a button on the stick.

Starting *Stiletto* is standard Mustang throttle cracked mixture idle cut-off, fuel pump on, engage starter, mags on, prime, mixture up when running on prime. Once running turn on the water pump for the spray bar, and turn on the computer and set desired temperatures. It cools fine on the ground, but once the temperatures are up it takes a lot of spray bar water to maintain temperatures, therefore ground time is kept to a minimum. Taxiing is straight forward P-51, very easy with the steerable tail wheel.

The only problem is the canopy can't be opened while taxiing so S turns must be exaggerated to clear the area in front. This is the only area that is uncomfortable when flying the aircraft. The bubble is small and there's not much room to move your head. Runup is stock

P-51. All the trim tabs are operated electrically, with the elevator and aileron trim controlled by the coolie hat on the stick, and a toggle switch on the left console controls the rudder trim. Trim is set visually as there are no indicators in the cockpit. For normal flight,trim is set at neutral, except for right rudder trim. Nose down trim is used takeoff when racing, due to 40 gallons of ADI behind the pilot.

Takeoff power is 61 inches and 3000 RPM, the aircraft tends to swing left but is easily controlled with right rudder. The tail comes up at about 70 mph and at this point visibility is much improved. Because of the racing nose gears the acceleration on takeoff is slightly less than a stock Mustang. It flies off in a tail low attitude between 135-160 mph depending on weight and attitude. The landing gear must be retracted quickly to avoid overspeeding the gear speed of 170 mph.

As in any Mustang temperatures must be monitored closely to confirm that the automatic systems are performing correctly. A climb speed of between 220-250 mph is used when going cross country, climb power is set at 46 inches and 2700 rpm's.

In flight characteristics are exceptional; in fact at cruise it is more stable than a stock Mustang. Once trimmed, it will fly hands off for short periods of time. Ailerons begin to stiffen as speed increases. Elevators are light compared to the ailerons, and remain light even at race speeds and above. After about 200 mph, elevator trim is not needed and the aircraft stays in trim from 200-500 mph indicated. Visibility is very good

in cruise and at high speed flight. It's extremely hard to slow to gear speed of 170 mph, a combination of flaps and power reduction will slow the aircraft. To give an example of how clean *Stiletto* really is we flew it in formation with a Fouga Magister jet, lowered the noses and leaving the power alone *Stiletto* pulled away from the jet.

As the airplane slows the small ailerons become progressively sloppier. The aircraft can be slowed to 105 mph dirty, apply full T.O. power 61 inches and 3000 rpm without rolling on it's back, rudder is the key, if it is not used it will roll over (just like a stocker). Stalls are more docile with good warning although faster than a stock P-51. It lacks the tendency to drop a wing in unaccelerated or accelerated flight.

Clean, power off, stall speed is 110mph, dirty with full flaps and gear down power off is 98 mph, with power on dirty it stalls at 103mph, we believe the reason for a higher stall speed with power on is because of all the right rudder and aileron required. Stall recovery is immediate with relaxation of back pressure.

With gear and full flaps down, approach speed is kept at 150mph on final, slowing to 125 mph across the fence, with throttle brought back to idle in the flair or a long float will result. Often we'll pull the mixture on the ground to help reduce the ground roll. The tail comes down at about 90 mph and forward visibility becomes nil. Rollout is very straight forward like a stock Mustang.

Probably the most difficult thing racing at Reno is finding the pylons. Generally, you see the cars parked around the pylons, then spot the pylons. The only time on the course to get a little breather is between pylons 3 and 4, going away from the crowd. The last pylon (No.8), comes up the quickest, is hard to see and is one of the tightest on the course.

Alan Preston whom we bought *Stiletto* from is the man responsible for *Stiletto* being built. He and Bruce Lockwood also played a large part in *Stiletto* being at Reno this year. Both pitched in and helped us get the airplane in the air and race ready. Alan also made available his trailer at Reno for us to use.

GOLD RACE ON SUNDAY

Our race strategy was to run the whole race with as little power as possible, while staying within striking distance of the leader, hoping to pass on the last lap. We were prepared to run whatever power was necessary, on the last lap, to win on Sunday.

The race proceeded as normal, with all aircraft taking off in order and joining the pace airplane, flown by Bob Hoover. This part of the race is quite an experience. Looking out of the tiny bubble canopy at all the fastest Unlimiteds in line abreast formation, the view is breathtaking. After years of watching these famous racers from the ground, to be alongside was

Stiletto - Reno 1986 - the clipped wings and pushed-back cockpit seen to good effect (Gruening)

unimaginable.

Bob Hoover leads the racers down onto the course and with those famous words 'Gentlemen you have a race' the race is on. This is a busy time for all the pilots. Power is added, engine parameters and systems are monitored along with looking for the next pylon and the other traffic.

As we came down the chute all systems were go. 'Tiger' Bill Destefani in *Strega* and Rick Brickert in *Dreadnought* jumped into the lead. They were followed closely by Lyle Shelton in *Rare Bear* and *Stiletto*.

Soon after the start of the first lap, we passed *Rare Bear* and continued to pursue the leaders. Rick Brickert and Tiger Destefani really put on a show for the record crowd, passing the lead back and forth several times. We continued to run as planned, slightly behind the leaders (thinking they might break). The engine was running very smoothly and all the temperatures and pressures looked good. So we were confident we would have ample power to pass at the end of the race. Then on lap 4, I got an indication of a problem when passing pylon 5. The engine missed for just a second, all the gauges were in green, and I wasn't sure what the problem might be. So it being the Gold race on Sunday, we of course continued to race.

The race is flown between 50-150 feet off the ground. For the most part the highest G load on the pylon turns is about 5. The cockpit lacks ventilation (ie. Drag), so even though it's not hot it does get a bit warm for circulation. Workload in *Stiletto* is minimal, as far as engine cooling and systems go. Being fully automated, the pilot only has to monitor the gauges in front of him along with a few idiot highlights. As the race unfolded the engine continued to miss intermittently. We were still turning laps in the high 440's with low power. When we passed the

white flag with one lap to go the engine backfired loudly, and immediately got pretty rough. I assumed the engines had detonated and prepared for the worst. I eased the nose up, brought the power back and shut the engine down with the mixture. We still gained about 4000'AGL. I shut down the ADI and water pumps, and set up for a forced landing. Fortunately there was no oil on the windshield so we just pointed toward the nearest runway. With the runway made, flaps were extended to reduce speed. With no power, not wanting to slow to gear speed, the gear was lowered at 200 mph about 1000'AGL. Touchdown was at 150 mph, and rollout was normal although very quiet.

Of course we were all disappointed that we hadn't won, but we certainly had fun. Besides it's not so bad when you get beat by a couple of great competitors, not to mention true gentlemen like Tiger Destefani, Rick Brickert and Alan Preston.

We were also very lucky in because the engine wasn't hurt. The rocker nut backed off and let the valve close, which caused the backfire. My brother test flew the airplane the next day for an hour, and after pulling the screens and checking it over, flew it home to Florida two days later.

Quite a few people have asked how we as newcomers were treated. We can only say that we were treated extremely well, all the pilot and crews couldn't have been more professional, or treated us any better. We came from Reno with great respect for all the pilots and crews, who welcomed us rookies with open arms. Everyone we worked with were always there with a helping hand or a word of advice, making it a very enjoyable experience. **WW Scott Sherman.**

Old Flying Machine Company Mustang

Now with the Old Flying Machine Company, CAC Mustang A68-192 is seen here in 1963 as VH-FCB (A.P.N. via Gary Brown).

Platinum Plus

Just before his untimely death in the Unlimited air racer Tsunami, John R. Sandberg, one of the co-founders of Warbirds Worldwide, had this ex Dominican Mustang, 44-72051/N68JR completely rebuilt by the Chino based Fighter Rebuilders. The entire airframe was completely reskinned. A full feature appeared on this aircraft in Warbirds Worldwide Number 18. A colour plate of the aircraft appears on page 82. Photographs by Frank Mormillo (Top) and Alan Gruening (Below)

Gary Brown and **James Kightly** detail an increasingly healthy European Mustang population

With the end of the war in Europe, the Allies turned their attention to Japan and the resident U.S.A.A.F. units quickly regrouped in anticipation of moving to the Far East or a return to the U.S. Almost overnight, the legendary Mustang disappeared from Europe with most of the aircraft returning home and only a handful of airframes remaining - some being held in storage depots around the United Kingdom for eventual disposal. Many others were damaged and classified as beyond economical repair. These were later scrapped. Eventually, several Mustangs, some of them Eighth Air Force airframes, survived this debacle following purchase by Sweden, Switzerland, and Italy who were energetically re-equipping their post war air forces.

With the emergence of the jet engine during the 1950s the reliable, though now out-performed P-51 was nearing the end of it's sojourn into Europe. Many were relegated to training duties and eventually disposed of. Some airframes were destined for the smelter with others going further afield to equip the fledgling air arms of developing nations. In 1958 when the last surviving Swiss Air Forces P-51Ds were scrapped a fifteen year period of continuous Mustang activity ended in Europe. (In the Middle East, as we shall see, the Israeli Defence Forces still held some P-51s on strength until the 1960s).

It was to be six long years before the Mustang returned to European skies. However in this period there were to be a couple of notable false starts. In the early 60's the *United Dominions Trust* of London purchased a Commonwealth Aircraft Corporation CA17 Mk.A68-5 (registered VH-BVM) in Australia. Unfortunately, while en-route to the U.K. the aircraft (registered G-ARKD) suffered a cockpit fire while at Athens in September 1961. G-ARKD was abandoned and subsequently became derelict, it's final fate unknown.

Just under two years later, Ron Flockhart of Melbourne, Australia purchased A68-173, then registered VH-UWB from *Brookes Aviation* at Moorabbin. Tragically, only eight days after Flockhart placed the aircraft on the British civil register as G-ARUK he was killed in the Mustang while on a final approach to land near Kalistra, Victoria on the 12th of April 1962. It is thought the aircraft was intended for use in the U.K.

1964 finally saw a P-51 return to Europe with the arrival of N6356T (44-74494) in Luxembourg after a transatlantic ferry flight from La Porte, Indiana carried out by Bill Rolfe. After a brief period of operation in Luxembourg while owned by *Interocean Airways*, N6356T, an ex-Royal Canadian Air Force P-51D Mustang was purchased by Charles Masefield, who was the Chief Test pilot for the Beagle Aircraft Company. From it's base at Shoreham on the Sussex coast, Masefield regularly flew the aircraft at airshows and air races including the 1967 King's Cup held at Tollerton. (which he won). After a complicated series of ownership manoeuvres before and after the *Patton - Lust for Glory* movie (See WW18), which saw Masefield's period of ownership finish, N6356T was sold to Ed Jurist of New York and the aircraft returned to the U.S.A. in early 1971.

During the period of 1968-71, Europe had two airworthy Mustangs when Cavalier Mustang N6851D passed through Shannon, Ireland during December '68 while en-route to it's new owner; Ditta Billi of Florence, Italy. After acquisition from Cavalier (Jerry Tyler of Ellenton Florida, U.S.A.was the ferry pilot) the aircraft, 44-74694, was placed on the Italian civil register appropriately as I-BILL.

Top: *One of the first real American warbirds to fly in the UK. Seen on the ramp at Gander, Newfoundland in the summer of 1964 is N6356T. Overall colour is white with a thin red cheatline. (Keith Houston).*

Airworthy Mustangs in Europe

After almost ten years of ownership, Ditta sold the aircraft to Ormond Haydon Baillie who had already amassed a considerable aircraft collection based at Duxford in Cambridgeshire. Haydon Baillie stole the show when he brought the aircraft into the UK for the last day of the 1977 I.A.T. airshow at Greenham Common. However, on the third of July 1977 O.H.B. was killed along with a passenger and I-BILL destroyed when the aircraft crashed on take off after an airshow at Mainz-Finthen in Germany.

During 1977 a remarkable visit was made by P-51D NL5747 to Europe. Pilot Robert Bladon with owner Tony Ostermeir flew the Atlantic (using F-86 Sabre wing tanks) via the northern route transiting through Greenland, Iceland and finally arriving at Prestwick in Scotland. The aircraft reached Duxford Airfield during the evening of the 16th of June, just in time to display at the weekend's Silver Jubilee Airshow. After a brief excursion around the European continent the Mustang then returned to the U.S. It was destroyed on 4th October 1980 following a post-rebuild crash.

With the demise of I-BILL and the tragic loss of it's owner, Europe was again lacking an active Mustang. During this time Doug Arnold was rapidly establishing a vast collection of warbirds at Blackbushe Airfield in Surrey. In 1979 Mr.Arnold's *Warbirds of Great Britain* received P-51D N166G (ex-44-63788) which was ferried to the U.K.in company with Republic P-47 N47DE. (Before leaving the U.S.A. N166G had survived a tornado that hit the Bradley Air Museum). The Mustang was placed on the British civil register as G-PSID and was repainted in an R.A.F. colour scheme.

During it's period with W.O.G.B. the aircraft made a number of airshow appearances, and appeared statically in the film *Eye of the Needle*. Eventually G-PSID was sold to the Fighter Collection and joined the *Old Flying Machine Company's* C.A.C. Mustang and the *Fighter Collection's* other P-51D for the filming (in Spain) of the aerial sequences for *Empire of the Sun* where it was named *Tugboat* and painted in the colours of the 118th Tactical Reconnaissance Squadron, 23rd Fighter Group of the 14th Air Force. Soon after filming it was sold to Jean Salis of La Ferte Alais, France, and re-registered F-AZFI. It is shown today in a more permanent version of it's film colours as *Empire of the Sun*.

On the 6th of May 1980 the wheels of North American P-51D Mustang N6340T touched the runway at Lucerne in Switzerland. The Mustang was back in Europe; and this time the Mustang was here to stay. N6340T's long range tanks would not be needed to take the aircraft back across the Atlantic like it's predecessors. In 1980 Stephen Grey of The Fighter Collection acquired P-51D N6340T. This ex-Mojave air racer has since become a cornerstone of the Duxford based Fighter Collection. During April of 1981 the aircraft relinquished it's all over red racing colour scheme. Repainting was carried

Top: Another shot of '56T when it was based in the UK and wearing race number 100. Pictured here at Shoreham on 20th May 1968 (S.C. Reglar). Below: The ill-fated Mustang G-ARKD in Athens shortly before a fire caused significant damage. The ultimate fate of the substantial remains is unknown (B.N. Stainer). Bottom: Shot during a visit to the UK from the U.S.A. the ill fated Mustang Pilot's Club N5747/44-73027 (G.R. Brown Collection)

out at Heathrow and favoured the modified 357thFG 362ndFS markings of Lt. *Moose* Myron Becraft. The aircraft retained the racing name of *Candyman* bestowed by it's racing owner Charles Beck on the starboard side of it's nose. Stephen Grey has always been a regular participant at airshows all over Europe; initially Ray Hanna undertook many the Mustang's show commitments including the aircrafts European debut at the 1981 Biggin Hill Air Fair.

It was later re-registered N51JJ .

Moose has been a heavy participant in the European film scene, appearing as *My Dallas Darlin"* in *Empire of the Sun* and as itself (but coded AJ-S *Candyman/Moose* in *Memphis Belle*. On August 9th 1990, the Mustang was unfortunate enough to make a wheels up landing at Stapleford. Though the damage was not serious, it was ironic that *Moose* had only just finished a total rebuild part of which consisted

of a revision to a stock cockpit instrument panel. The engine runs and test flight had taken place on the morning of the year's *Classic Fighter Display* at Duxford. Recently, due to a shift in registrations to the U.K. by several warbird operators *Moose* has been re-registered in the U.K. G-BTCD.

Throughout the early 1980's Ray Hanna was regularly flying Stephen Grey's P-51 at displays and many other warbirds around the world. When Ray Hanna and Mark Hanna formed *The Old Flying Machine Company* in 1981, a P-51 was high on their 'wants' list. Meanwhile in Hong Kong, a Commonwealth Aircraft Corporation built C.A.C. Mk22 A68-192 was in store.

Acquired by Ray in the mid 1970s, and unloaded from a Boeing 747F at Gatwick airport on 28th of February 1985 the U.K. registered G-HAEC was taken to Duxford where it has been based ever since. This Mustang was to be destined for a hard working life with starring roles in *Empire of the Sun* as 592 *Missy Wong from Hong Kong, Memphis Belle* as AJ-A *Ding Hao* (the scheme it wears today).

A long chain of events had lead to the aircraft becoming a resident of Hong Kong. After ser-

Top: *Stephen Grey during air testing of Mustang G-BTCD from Duxford in the Autumn of 1991 (John Dibbs).* ***Left:*** *The late Pierre Dague enjoyed flying the French based, Salis Mustang F-AZFI seen here at La Ferte Alais May 1991.(James Kightly)*

vice with the Royal Australian Air Force the aircraft was placed onto the civil register in 1959 as VH-FCB. In 1964 the machine was given a very striking racing scheme of red, black and white for the Ansett sponsored Brisbane to Adelaide air race, the Mustang being placed first in the speed section.

After rising operating costs, it was stored in the Philippines in 1969. Then registered PI-C-561 the aircraft suffered several mishaps during it's time in the Philippines including an alarming engine failure; the subsequent dead-stick landing seeing the aircraft strike a lamp standard on it's final approach! In 1976 the Mustang was transported to Hong Kong for an eventual rebuild. As a regular visitor to Hong Kong in his (then) profession as a pilot for *Cathay Pacific* airlines, Ray Hanna had noticed the presence of this Mustang in store on the island. Ray purchased the aircraft with a view to a long term restoration being done by the *Hong Kong Aircraft Engineering Company* under the supervision of Mal Rose. The Mustang bug was to bite hard on the continent as well as in England. Switzerland, having seen *Moose* based in the U.K. later saw the import of N51EA (44-72483)by *Swiss Warbirds* and painted as *Double Trouble Two.* Sold by Don Davidson of Nashua, New Hampshire, the aircraft was air-ferried to Basel in Switzerland, in the hands of Max Vogelsang and Swiss Aerobatics Champion Christian Schweizer, arriving on August 26 1990 (ten years after the arrival of Moose!).See the article on Page 45. With a striking black and yel-

low chequered nose, N51EA was to debut in the U.K., at where else but the 1991 *Classic Fighter Display* at Duxford. A European Mustang that remained this side of the Atlantic since the war was 44-63864, serving initially with the 78th Fighter Group 83rd Fighter Squadron as *Twilight Tear* where in the hands of Lt. Hubert Davis it was to score two kills. It was sent to Sweden in 1949, and then passed to the Israeli Defence Forces in 1953. It was bought by Israeli Itzhaki who restored the aircraft to airworthy condition in Israel, the all important flight taking place on 5th of February 1984. The aircraft ended up with *Novida* AB as SE-BKG, based at Malmo, arriving in December 1986, where it is painted in an authentic Flgvapnet scheme as

Above: A regular visitor to the UK is the Scandinavian Historic Flight's P-51D N167F which was restored by Darrell Skurich (James Kightly). Below: Film star Ding Hao unsticks from the runway at Duxford (John Dibbs).

FvNr 26158.

In 1980 Mustang N167F was flown by it's owner Paul D. Finefrock to Darrell Skurich's *Vintage Aircraft Ltd*, of Fort Collins Colorado for restoration, but whilst the aircraft was there Finefrock decided to sell. Darrell contacted Anders K. Saether of the *Scandinavian Historic Flight* who was looking for a good condition Mustang .

44-73877 fitted the bill admirably, though it needed a full restoration to meet Anders high

standards. Due to the nature of the environ- ment N167F was expected to operate in i.e. Scandinavia and the U.K., a full modern cock- pit fit was installed with I.F.R. and modern avionics.

After a *Hovey Machine Products* Merlin was fit- ted, the aircraft was flown to Arden Fisher in San Antonio Texas for painting in the colours of Captain Bud Anderson's *Old Crow*; Chuck Yeager's wingman in the 357th FG. (See WW15). In 1986, after Anders had been checked out on the essentially new Mustang he flew it to Norway, where it is now based. A regular visitor to the U.K - participating in the *Memphis Belle* filming as *Cisco* (coded AJ-N). Interestingly, dur- ing the initial stages of filming *Cisco* acquired two bird kill markings under the cockpit along- side the more conventional score. Sadly *Enigma Productions* asked for them to be removed, as they compromised the aircraft's scheme. N167F reverted to it's *Old Crow* colours after filming ended, and was totally resprayed in a slightly different colour silver.

Registered as N9772F for it's ferry flight from Israel to Le Bourget for the Musee del'Air et l'Espace, 44-63871 was only briefly an airwor- thy European Mustang, it now being displayed statically at that French museum.

France now has a second airworthy Mustang in the form of F-AZMU *Jumpin Jaques* which is an ex Colombian aircraft. Bought by Jaques Bourett and based at Rambert St. D'Albon, reg- istered to *Aero Retro*, 44-72035 was flown by

Jaques in a temporary silver and blue scheme for the May 1989 La Ferte Alais Show. It is now

Like many other European based P-51s, G- SUSY (named after owner Charles Church's wife) flew to great Britain via the North Atlantic, in this case piloted by Jack Shaver, flying via Newfoundland and Iceland arriving in the U.K. on the 26th of June 1987. Used by the Nicaraguan Air Force after it's service with the Texas Air National Guard, this airframe, 44- 72773, passed through a selection of U.S. owners before being sold to Charles Church by Robert Ferguson. Like most of the available U.K. population G-SUSY participated in the *Memphis Belle* film being painted as AJ-C - a scheme it wears in a modified form today .The aircraft was recently sold to Paul Baker and is currently based at North Weald.

Registered as N1051S to George Sullivan in 1970, this P-51D Mustang (45-11371) was to come to the U.K. to revitalise well known col- lector Spencer Flack's interest in Warbirds. Registered to *Myrick Aviation* and painted in 4th FG colours as *Sunny VIII*, N1051S arrived by air in the U.K. at Southend on the evening of 22nd June 1987, in the hand of Ward Wilkins and Ray Middleton (just preceding G-SUSY) from where it went onto regular airshow displays and a walk on part in it's original colours in *Memphis Belle*, having been bought from it's last owner, Jimmie R. MacMillan of Breckenridge, Texas. It was for many years owned by Peter MacManus and based in Florida in a civilian type paint scheme.

Imported to the UK by Charles Church (Spitfires) Limited in June 1987, N12066 was quickly registered G-SUSY, though it main- tained this paint scheme for some time before being painted for use in the film Memphis Belle. Currently based at North Weald, G-SUSY is currently owned by Paul J. Morgan. Pictured here at West Malling soon after it arrived in the UK (Gary R. Brown)

When Peter acquired another Mustang, N1051S was sold on and eventually purchased by Jimmie who undertook a total rebuild com- plete with a *Vintage V-12s* Merlin.

Despite the sale of G-PSID, Doug Arnold had not bowed out of Mustang operations, as the P-51D N314BG 44-73140 arrived at Biggin Hill during 1988 resplendent in the colours of John Meyer, C.O. of the 352nd Fighter Group as *Petie 2nd*. This almost zero-timed Mustang had been restored by *Pioneer Aero* in the U.S. The same company were also commissioned to rebuild two more Mustangs for *Warbirds of Great Britain* and these are covered adequately in the article on *Pioneer Aero*. They were due to arrive in the UK in February 1992.

Possibly the most unusual European Mustang, G-BIXL did not come to the U.K. by the usual warbird U.S. - Atlantic route, being the only Mustang that was totally restored to airworthy condition in the U.K. so far. In 1976 Robs Lamplough, then part of the naissant U.K.warbird scene was scouring the world for Mustangs suitable for restoration. In Israel he struck gold finding three suitable aircraft, including I.D.F. '43' an ex Swedish A.F. machine, which he chose to restore and registered as G-BIXL. 44-72216 was another ex-Eighth Air Force machine being flown by Captain Raymond Littge as HO-L *The Silver Dollar* who scored several kills in the aircraft and as *Miss Nita* by Russell H. Ross who flew it until the wars end. Importing the three airframes into the U.K. in 1978 restoration commenced on them by various groups. After several years and a move while under restoration from Duxford to North Weald, 'XL finally took to the air again on the 5th of May 1987 in the hands of Mark Hanna. G-BIXL took part in *Memphis Belle* where it was on occasion flown by Pete John.

Robs Lamplough had also bought N51RR from Ron Runyan with the aim of competing with it at the 1990 Reno Air Races (the aircraft having previously competed as racer '51) but due to red tape was unable to do so in 1990. Restored by Ron and *Fighter Rebuilders*, 44-74008 was ferried to the U.K. in 1991, joining a now extensive range of European Mustangs. Robs, already owner of G-BIXL, sold N51RR to Dave Gilmour who had the aircraft ferried to the U.K. It has now begun to slot into the U.K. scene appearing at *The Fighter Meet* at North Weald, Duxford's *Classic Fighter* 1991 (where it was flown by Norman Lees) and also at R.F.C. *Rendcomb's* initial display on September 15th 1991.

And waiting in the wings? Robert Lamplough recovered several Mustangs on his various forays into Israel, and one, IDF 41 was sold to Noel Robinson. Noel and his team are hard at work on this long term project at Tees-side airport, and there has been significant progress in recent times. The aircraft serial number has been traced as 44-72028 which also makes this an ex 8th Air Force airframe. The group have manufactured several major sub-assemblies in house to exceptionally high standards including several doghouse sections, some of which they hope to pass on in exchange for other parts to advance the whole project. Another area they are currently examining is the complex airscoop section.

Another project that received little publicity was an ex Indonesian TNI-AU airframe purchased from the late Stephen Johnson by Chris Warrillow of Wooburn Green, Buckinghamshire. 44-73543 was imported as a 'starter kit' from the United States and was later registered G-BLYW. Though some work was completed Chris decided to sell the aircraft to D.K. Precision who registered it as N800DK in April 1986.

So while we are unlikely to see again the massed formations of P-51s riding shotgun on the 8th Air Force bomber formations, groups of four or more Mustangs are by no means rare in Europe, and it seems to be an expanding population, a reflection perhaps, of a healthy worldwide trend. It seems that in Europe this time the Mustangs are here to stay. **WW James Kightly and Gary Brown.**

Top: G-SUSY again, this time in olive drab and at Duxford, post *Memphis Belle* filming *(Richard Paver)*. *Below:* registered as N51RR/44-74008 under final assembly by Fighter Rebuilders at Chino in California. Ron Runyan began the rebuild but it was taken over by Fighter Rebuilders in the final stages. *Bottom:* An indication of the number of Mustangs in Europe - the line up at Duxford for the fighter sequences of *Memphis Belle (Gary Brown)*

Twin Stick TEMCO

Paul Coggan writes up the story of John MacGuire's original TEMCO TF-51D.
Pictures courtesy **Darrell Skurich**

Top: *Early 1985 and the Vintage V-12's Merlin fires into life for the first set of engine runs in the Colorado snow. The longer TF-51D canopy, which is enlarged both in length and height to accommodate the rear pilot, is shown to advantage in this picture. This particular Mustang served with the Indiana Air National Guard as 44-84658.* **Lower:** *now completely cowled, Don Whittington prepares the aircraft for its first flight and subsequent test flight programme. Only minor faults showed during the programme and these were quickly rectified before John MacGuire took delivery of the rare machine. (Vintage Aircraft Limited).*

Vintage Aircraft Limited

Vintage Aircraft Limited of Fort Collins, Colorado, have been covered in various editions of *Warbirds Worldwide*. The company was founded by Darrell Skurich - and they specialise in exceptionally high quality restorations to owners specifications. Amongst the more famous Mustangs rebuilt by *Vintage Aircraft* are the *Scandinavian Historic Flight's* P-51D N167F - the subject of a previous article in *Warbirds Worldwide* 15 and our back cover photograph, as well as the *Experimental Aircraft Associations's* unique and original North American XP-51, now in the EAA *Museum* at Oshkosh in Wisconsin after it was grounded due to its rarity.

One of the lesser known projects tackled by *Vintage Aircraft* is the North American TF-51D N51TF-44-84658. This aircraft was purchased by John MacGuire from the late Stephen Johnson and was an ex TNI-AU (Indonesian Air Force) Cavalier TF-51D. It flew with the code F-361 with the Indonesians, and is a genuine original TEMCO version - the fourth of fifteen twin stick Mustangs modified from a Texas batch of P-51D-25NTs. Whilst many standard Mustangs were modified in the field with two control sticks and rear cockpit skeleton instrumentation, the TEMCO aircraft had two cockpits separated by a centre console.

When the aircraft arrived at Fort Collins it was in very poor shape according to Darrell -'all of the dual control parts were missing....'.

Work began in November 1983 with the uncrating of the airframe and a general survey to determine exactly what was required. Basically the TF-51 was just a shell. New longerons were installed for starters, and as can be seen from the accompanying pictures the centre fuselage section was completely stripped and inspected during this process. The longerons (the four main extrusions which run the length of the centre fuselage section) are no different for the TF than the standard Mustang.

From here, once the basic centre section is complete, the rest of the aircraft starts to be built around it. Though its sounds remarkably simple, the same process is undertaken on the wings. The fuselage was extensively reskinned. All the dual control parts were manufactured by *Vintage Aircraft* '...there was nothing difficult....' says Darrell 'it just takes time.'

All new hydraulic lines were manufactured and fitted and the TF was completely rewired with all new electrical components. *Vintage V-12's* produced the engine for the project. After approximately 4500 hours of work Don Whittington put the Mustang through the flight test programme in early 1985.

Rather than produce an in depth word laden article on this particular Mustang we thought a pictorial article would best show the amount and standard of work involved in the rebuild of N51TF. **WW Paul Coggan**

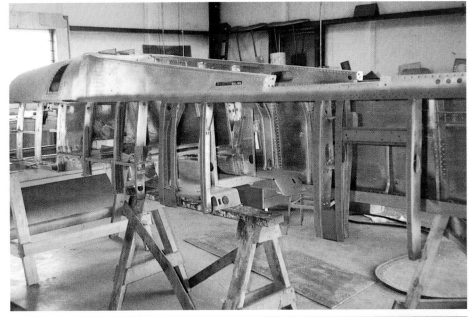

*Top: Two ex Indonesian Mustangs arrived at Fort Collins for rebuild - N51TF is on the right hand side. As can be seen from the photograph the shell was in poor condition. **Below:** work underway. Approximately 4500 hours were spent on the rebuild of N51TF - the fuselage is seen undergoing longeron replacement. Note how clean the metalwork is. **Bottom:** rotating dolly allows access to all parts of the fuselage during the rebuild process (Vintage Aircraft)*

El Salvador's Mustangs

The Fuerza Aerea Salvadorena operated some 19 recorded Mustangs including one dual control TF-51D (FAS400). Of the nineteen airframes the majority were delivered from the United States in 1969 - the top up for a previous order from Cavalier of seven aircraft (including the single TF-51D). Shown here are *(top)* N30FF - which is now with Butch Schroeder in Danville, Illinois and *(lower)* N32FF which is 44-73656was later sold to Chris Williams of Ellensburg, Washington. A further group of aircraft are shown opposite *(top)* prior to their leaving El Salvador and *(lower)* N34FF (which became N51WE with Bill Clark-who was killed in it on 7th March 1988) foreground and N32FF at the back. All Photographs via Dick Phillips.

The Best Years of Our Lives

It was during the preparation of this latest *Warbirds Worldwide* title that it suddenly occurred to me that I had in many ways been involved with researching the P-51 for the past 20 years. This realisation was *not* a pleasant experience!

So I hope you will allow me the indulgence of making a few comments on the story so far, and to reflect upon some personal experiences and some memories of acquaintances made over the last 20 years, with regard to the type.

My interest, as recorded before elsewhere, in the P-51 was kindled by the arrival (and subsequent display at a Rolls-Royce airshow at Hucknall in Nottinghamshire - an airfield itself steeped in history) of Mustang N6356T in the UK. I could not help but be impressed when it arrived - in its beautiful blood red paint scheme - in formation with nine Folland Gnats of the Red Arrows. Perhaps you will not believe me when I tell you I did not know what it was! However, the sound, the shape captured my imagination. I was not only hooked but I was captivated with the aircraft that I have to admit later became an obsession. Just a few weeks later, when seeing my uncle leave for Canada on a BOAC Boeing 707 from Manchester Ringway airport I saw a copy of Air Pictorial at the local bookshop - and Charles Masefield flying the magnificent red Mustang on the cover. That was it.

For some years the Mustang bug lay dormant in my system. I went through a fairly basic edu-

> **Paul Coggan** reflects on the last twenty years of his interest in Mustangs, the people he has met and the changing times.

cation, preferring studying aviation to revising for important school exams. For my sins I joined the RAF at age 16 in 1973. Work and training in Air Traffic Control took up most of my time.

However, just before I left Wittering for RAF Watton and Eastern Radar my interest in the

Mustang emerged again. A previous contact with Harry Holmes at what was then Hawker Siddeley Woodford (as an eight year old I used to spot HS748's on test flights from Woodford, listen to their radio transmissions on a small VHF radio, get their callsigns and write to Harry

Keith Houston sent in this photograph recently **(top)** *and it hardly seems more than 20 years since it was in the UK with Charles Masefield. Below: Israel was the source of several airframes including this one* **(below)** *fairly recently rebuilt and painted as N471R 'The Huntress'. (Eddie Toth Photograph).*

Reg Urschler in the C.A.F.'s Gunfighter alias N5428V (Eddie Toth)

for more details!) later turned into a mutual interest in the Mustang. I produced my first typed master listing of surviving Mustangs after several months of research (largely into other researchers articles and files) and Harry kindly made comments, and I revised the list, later sending it on to other more respected researchers. The more I delved the more interested I became - and the more people I came into contact with.

I was then introduced to Dick Phillips, in turn to the late Malcolm Gougon, Bill Larkins (who was always generous with information from his files and photographic archive) and many other people. After securing a list of current Mustangs and their owners I wrote to them all with the idea of starting up an international association of Mustang people; Enthusiasts. owners, rebuilders - indeed anyone with a serious interest in the P-51.

The idea blossomed, and my interest moved from historical research into recording what was happening to the type today. This was so important, and yet no one really seemed to be taking that much notice of what was happening to the aircraft right now!

One of my first letters was to Dr. Burns M. Byram who at the time owned Mustang N51N alias 44-73140. I was upset when I received a reply from his secretary informing me Burns had been killed in a Mustang crash in Mexico (whilst ferrying N52HA an ex FAG aircraft) to the USA. She did say that he would have been very interested in my intentions to launch Mustang International. It was 9th June 1978.

Mustang International began with a regular newsletter, the first of which was produced by Jerry Scutts (a much respected researcher and author) and photocopied by a local print shop. It went down very well. Congratulations came in from various sources and the membership grew. The photocopied newsletter grew too, and soon became an obsession. I was also working in the RAF though my roster allowed for much correspondence and research, which sadly has decreased in more recent times. Introductions to Jerry Vernon and Jeff Ethell followed. M.I. continued to flourish. Contact after contact with Mustang owners came in, and it was here I came into contact with Butch Schroeder and later John Sandberg.

As M.I. grew I eventually made contact with Gordon Plaskett. At this time Plaskett was, as far as I was concerned carrying the callsign Golf Oscar Delta One as far as Mustangs were concerned. And who was this guy with the unpronounceable name Zeuschel who I was to have the occasional in depth conversation with? Dave certainly set me straight about my next obsession. Aircraft identities. Paperwork, said Dave "is the bottom of the priority list when it comes to rebuilding Mustangs" He advised that whilst private research was fine, actually reporting some of the serial numbers might not be totally advisable. I was later to find that several aircraft were not what their paperwork said they were and that newer rebuilds generally utilised the nearest hulk. It did not make them any less airworthy, or of poorer quality. But no-one shouted about it. It is, thank goodness, becoming more important today and owners are more interested in the history of their aircraft. I like to think that this has a little to do with prompting from Mustang International, and more recently its successor, Warbirds Worldwide.

The next turning point came with an introduction to Robert Lamplough who had just recovered several Mustangs from Israel. It was Robs that would encourage me to take on the rebuild of one of these aircraft. I later formed the RAF Watton Mustang Restoration Group. We never did finish IDF 28 but the work we did do certainly would have prolonged the airframes life. And I learned a lot about the real world of warbird restoration. Then one day one of Robs German contacts asked me about IDF 28. I said it was basically a static rebuild. He scoffed. If it is not going to fly, why bother? Another turning point! To a certain extent I agreed. Norman Chapman was also working for Robs at the time. Norman was philosophical about rebuilding, but I could see how very different it was rebuild-

The Best Years of Our Lives

scheme details and Stephen offered me a trip in the P-51. Whilst at Watton I had been introduced to Robb Satterfield. We had corresponded for years (Robb owned a P-51D with Dallas Smith in Midland, Texas). Imagine my surprise when I arrived at Duxford to be told Robb may be taking me for the trip. But he was late.....would Steve Hinton do? Hinton? Golf Oscar Delta Two at the time. Stephen kindly introduced me -Fastest Piston pilot. Hinton started the walkaround. I tagged on like a schoolboy. Eventually, Robb turned up, and after several years of writing letters and 'phone conversations we met, face to face. What a gentleman. What a pilot. My first flight in a P-51 (Moose) with Robb up front was my first taste of high performance warbird flying. We were to fly to Wattisham where Mark Hanna was flying Phantoms in the RAF. Ray Hanna (also at the time pretty high up in the Golf Oscar Delta callsign table) was also flying in the Spitfire. Howard Pardue was flying the recently imported Corsair. We bounced Wattisham in a formation of Mustang (the only breach of camouflage being the glare from my teeth as I grinned from ear to ear - amidst resistance to blacking out from the G in the tight formation flying) P-40, P-47, Corsair and Spitfire. Only recently Robb passed on, a sad loss after a brave fight against cancer. How tragic after achieving so much in aviation, so many thousands of flying hours as a test pilot, warbird pilot, and aerobatic pilot too.

A few weeks later I was en route to the USA. I didn't know I was going to Oshkosh by Mustang. Fond Du where? Pete MacManus, Hess Bomberger, Bill Clark, Mark Clark, Denny Sherman - Jeff Ethell, Alan Preston. And Paul Poberezny (he shook my hand!). Johnny Baugh, Jimmy Leeward, Jimmie Hunt., Harry Tope. Twenty Six Flyable Mustangs. This was impossible. And who was this man and wife team?

ing a warbird to fly.

A few years later several Mustangs were recovered by Stephen Johnson of Oakland, California. I contacted him and he helped provide information on the serials. I also contacted a Rockwell representative in Indonesia who in turn put me in touch with the U.S. Defense Liaison Group there. Eventually Stephen himself became interested in the various aircraft's history. Sadly he was killed in an aircraft accident - whilst flying an N3N in California.

Some time later I received a letter from Butch Schroeder. Butch had acquired an F-6D. In a garage? Come on! Photographs followed. Butch suggested I visit him at Danville, and perhaps go to Oshkosh. I had wondered about this strange place in Wisconsin some years earlier, and had joined EAA and Warbirds of America some time previously. Meantime, the first flyable Mustang to come into Europe had been imported by Stephen Grey. I helped with colour

Top: I make no apology for publishing this fine view of two Mustangs that appeared on the front cover of our first special edition on the Mustang (Sherman Aircraft Sales). Another Mustang to inspire us - N6340T (now with The Fighter Collection) was one of the very first flyable Mustangs to be imported to Europe; seen here at Oakland, 27th June 1980 (Bill Larkins)

Flying Mustangs? Ed and Connie Bowlin. Mickey Rupp. Bob Pond, Kermit Weeks, Jim Fausz. The names of course were almost all recognisable to me after searching through so many Mustang history files. Mustang history, perhaps not of the 1940/50s variet but just as relevant. John Dilley, Moon and Dave Spillers. This was name dropping in the extreme. Canadians too! Dennis Bradley, Ross Grady. A Norwegian... yes - just took delivery of a Mustang from Darrell Skurich - Anders Saether. This was all too much. The sheer pleasure of meeting all these people was remarkable. To me what was even more remarkable was their congratulations on *Mustang International*. But we were only sending out a little photocopied newsletter (although it had grown into a reasonable 20 odd page booklet). But they loved it. Dick Phillips wanted me to meet John Sandberg. By the time I had moved toward the meeting place John had left to catch his flight to Minneapolis. Perhaps next year. Of course you know the rest of the story....

Several more visits to the USA, two of which were to work on inventory listings and advise the owners of several ex Dominican airframes on the rebuilds, to beautiful New Zealand, and Norway to see Mustangs; but most of all to meet some fantastic people. One of the high points, for me, was meeting Ed Horkey, who was Chief Aerodynamicist on the Mustang at North American Aviation. Ed is a wonderful character, still active and full of interesting stories. And then of course there was the guy from the little sleepy hollow at Dumbleton who would

telephone on exactly the day the newsletter was due. And he was just as important as the owners - Phillip Warner later became a firm supporter of *Warbirds Worldwide* and a good friend into the bargain.

Since then of course a lot has happened. Who would have said, in the early 1970's that the warbird movement would be so strong. The Mustangs are in good hands. The pilot attrition rate has been extremely painful, sometimes almost too hard to take. Some of the names I have mentioned, plus others, are no longer with us. Though I do believe that when a loss ceases to become painful I'll publish a book about skateboarding. The people we have lost - well they won't be forgotten. Sometimes too I have wavered a little. Spitfires - jets. What? Blow jobs? They're not real warbirds! You flew in a

what..........

When you examine the prospects today, and the values, things are not so bad. Before I became involved with warbirds people had told me that Mustang (and other warbird) owners could be a pretty arrogant bunch. They loved themselves. I can honestly say I have never come across one that fits that description yet. *Warbirds Worldwide* was founded in 1986 and continues to grow from strength to strength. If you are not a member how *can* you be seriously interested in warbirds?

Heard about the 25 P-51Bs they've just found in Russia? Or is it China? **WW Paul Coggan. Colour plates overleaf: N68JR - testimony to a man who insisted on the best, and to whom this book is dedicated; John R. Sandberg.**

A sad end for a distinguished old lady. Israeli Defence Force Mustang - it's not up there any more so don't book a flight! (**Robert Lamplough**)